True Crimes That Shaped Scotland Yard

James Tierney

DEDICATION

For May and Jimmy

CONTENTS

ACKNOWLEDGMENTS

With thanks to the National Library of Scotland for access to their extensive records.

1 WHATEVER HAPPENED TO HANNAH BROWN?

It was 28 December 1836 and Christmas was already becoming a fading memory as Constable Samuel Pegler of the London Police, South Division, was pounding the beat. Ten minutes after he'd heard the church clock strike two, the constable arrived in Edgware Road, where he was approached by an extremely agitated young man.

The man in question was labourer Robert Bond. Bond informed the policeman that on his way to work, he had stumbled upon what he believed was a human body tied up in a sack near the Pine Apple Gate in Edgware Road. The sack had been tied at the mouth when Bond had found it and natural curiosity had led him to open it. After his disbelieving eyes had focused on the hideous sight before him, he had quickly set off in search of a policeman.

The two men hastened to the scene, a public pathway about eighty yards from Pine Apple Gate. The sack was set, partly hidden from view, behind a large flagstone. Police-Constable Pegler carefully examined the course bag lying before him. Inside the sack did indeed lie the trunk of a human being. The head, thighs and legs had been hacked off and were nowhere to be seen. Lying beside the torso were blood-splattered pieces of old white linen cloth, some of which were patched over with nankeen. The arms of the corpse were tied, right arm over left, by a cord about the thickness of a common window sash cord. Grimly clinging to the interior of the sack was what looked to be fine scrapings of mahogany.

Pegler commandeered a wheelbarrow from a nearby allotment and conveyed the gruesome find directly to a neighbourhood workhouse in Paddington. Arrangements were swiftly made for the body to be examined by the local magistrate and the parish surgeon.

Shortly thereafter, a very brief Inquest was held and a verdict of 'wilful murder against some person or persons unknown' was recorded. The task of tracking down the perpetrator of the foul deed was placed in the capable hands of Inspector George Feltham of the Metropolitan Police, T-division.

At about 8:30am on the morning of 6 January 1837, Matthias Ralph, lock-keeper on the Regent's Canal, was in the process of opening the lock gates when a bargeman shouted to him that something was stuck in the gate. The lock-keeper grabbed a nearby boat-hook and set off to investigate. Ralph pushed the boat-hook firmly down into the water, then yanked at what he initially thought may be the body of a small dead dog trapped in the gate. As he began to raise the obstructing item, he was horrified to see it was, in fact, the head of a human being.

The water in that part of the canal was about five feet deep and just as Ralph was bringing the head to the surface, the boat-hook suddenly lost its grip and the head, with its long hair flowing gracefully behind, sunk back into the murky waters of the canal. Ralph eventually managed to get a firm grip on the hair and he twisted it around the boat-hook before pulling the head ashore.

The head, which could clearly be seen to be that of a woman, was missing the right eye. The jaw-bone was badly broken and had penetrated through the fair skin. The left ear looked like it had been torn at some stage as if an earring had been pulled forcefully from a piercing. The flesh, however, was in a near perfect state. Somewhat worryingly, based on his previous experiences of finding bodies in the water, Ralph was immediately able to estimate that the head had been in the water for four or five days.

Grim-faced, the lock-keeper raced to his house to fetch a length of cloth, which he carefully wrapped around the head. He then rushed the gruesome find to the bone-house of nearby Stepney Churchyard. Ralph locked the bone-house door behind him, returning the key to the grave-digger from whom he had borrowed it, before setting off to inform the authorities.

A local surgeon, John Birtwhistle, was urgently called out to examine the head. Birtwhistle noted that the head had received a savage blow to the right eye. The coats of the eye were ruptured and around the eye were signs of ecchymosis, the pouring out of the blood from the rupture of a vessel. That effect, the surgeon explained, would have been produced while the woman was alive and would have given the appearance of a tremendous black eye. There were several lacerations on the face, including a crescent-like laceration on the cheek, a contort wound on the lower jaw and a tear in the left ear. It was the surgeon's view that all the wounds except those on the eye and ear had been inflicted posthumously.

The head had been disjoined from the body at the fifth cervical vertebrae and it appeared the woman's throat had been cut while she had still been alive. The head was perfectly bloodless, an effect unlikely to have been produced if the throat had been cut after the woman was dead.

Following Birtwhistle's examination, the head was conveyed to the workhouse in Paddington where the body found at Pine Apple Gate was already located. The head and body fitted each other perfectly.

On the morning of 8 January 1837, three labourers were assigned the task of dragging the two-hundred-and-seventy-two yards of the Maida Hill Tunnel, one of three tunnels on the Regent's Canal, in the hope of locating the missing legs of the recently murdered woman. Watched by a crowd of curious bystanders, drawn like flies to the scene as the notoriety of the crime began to grow, the men worked until 2pm and had dragged an area stretching to about half-a-mile before they were forced to accept defeat.

The parish authorities and directors of the canal company then undertook to entirely drain a half-mile section of the Regent's Canal, between the Maida Hill Tunnel and Harrow-on-the-Hill, but this too proved to be unsuccessful.

As the intense search for the missing legs of the mystery woman continued, Inspector Feltham and Constable Pegler were engaged in a tireless attempt to identify her.

Feltham received a letter from a woman, Mrs Colburn from Elstree, who had read in the newspaper that there was a probability the murder had been committed by one of the canal boatmen. Colburn had recalled that a middle-aged woman of her acquaintance, Mrs Harris, had set off from Paddington, bound for Liverpool, on one of the canal boats on 22 December 1836. Harris had been accompanied to the boat by another woman, Mrs Bruce. Along with her luggage, Harris had taken a bottle of spirits and some ale. She had promised to write a letter to Mrs Bruce on her safe arrival in Liverpool, but no such letter had arrived.

The Inspector managed to track down Mrs Bruce quickly

and verified the story was true. Feltham quickly conveyed Mrs Bruce to the workhouse to view the murdered woman's head. After carefully examining the head, Mrs Bruce was of the opinion it was not the head of the woman in question.

Feltham thanked Mrs Bruce and immediately dispatched the letter he had received from Mrs Colburn to the police in Liverpool, asking them to make diligent inquiries with a view to ascertaining whether the woman had ever reached her destination. Mrs Harris was eventually traced and found to be safe.

Constable Pegler, meantime, was following up on information he'd received that the murdered woman was, without a shadow of a doubt, a Mrs Ricketts, who in September 1836 had left Willesden to collect a legacy of seven hundred pounds and had not been seen since. When the person who had provided this solid-gold information was taken to the workhouse in Paddington, they were unable to positively identify the head.

Feltham and Pegler switched their attention to questioning the sextons of nearby districts, with a view to ascertaining whether any graves had recently been disturbed and any female corpses removed. This line of inquiry also bore no fruit.

Fresh accounts of missing women were now arriving daily, yet no one had been able to confirm the identity of the murdered woman.

A decision was taken to preserve the head in spirits, to assist in identification, whilst the body would be interred.

On 2 February 1837, labourers James Page and Edward Brooks were hard at work in an osier bed in Coldharbour Lane, located between Camberwell and Brixton.

Page was ferreting for osiers among the bushes when he noticed there was a sack caught up in the undergrowth. As he dragged the sack into the open, Page noticed there was a hole in the bottom. Through the aperture, the two wide-eyed labourers could see what looked like part of a human knee and leg. The startled men hailed a passer-by, who provided them with directions to a nearby police station-house. Page set off at pace and soon returned to the scene in the company of Police Constable William Woodward and Police Inspector Bass.

The policemen looked through the hole in the sack and saw it contained two human legs and thighs, though, without disturbing the scene, they were unable to confirm whether the body parts were those of a woman.

Inspector Bass sent for a local surgeon, Mr Hammond, and upon his arrival, the sack, which was tied with a cord resembling a window-sash line, was cut open. The surgeon quickly confirmed the legs and thighs were those of a female.

The limbs were still fresh and white, although, from the appearance of the grass beneath where it had been found, the sack had lain on the spot for a considerable length of time. The surgeon estimated the limbs had been there for five or six weeks. The legs had been sawn off at the upper extremities of the thigh bones, partly sawn through then broken off. Hammond considered the saw was likely to have been a fine one, like that a butcher might use. The upper part of the thigh had been partly gnawed, probably by a rat. The limbs were bent in an acute angle, presumably to enable them to take up as little space as possible, and Hammond believed this must have been done immediately after death, while the body was still warm.

The sack had some visible lettering, printed in red capitals.

Part of a letter 'E', as well as the last five letters of a word ending 'R-W-E-L-L', could be clearly distinguished. A second word, containing the letters 'S-S-L-E-Y', could also be seen and Bass quickly realised the sack had at one time belonged to the brewers and coal merchants, Crossley's of Camberwell. Grimly gripping the bottom right-hand corner of the sack were some fine wood shavings.

After arranging for the body parts to be removed and taken to the workhouse in Paddington, the Inspector, based on the information he had gleaned from the sack, headed off to the house of Mr Crossley in Camberwell. Crossley agreed to accompany Bass to the station-house to examine the sack and he confirmed it had formerly been one of his. It would, he revealed, have been one of a consignment of forty he had ordered in 1834. He now had only one left in his possession and had no way of knowing where the other thirty-nine might have ended up, as they had been sent out with deliveries to retail sellers.

At the request of the parish officers, another surgeon, Mr Girdwood, was called in to inspect the limbs and provide a second opinion. He concurred with the findings of Hammond and confirmed, after minutely measuring all the relevant parts and examining the areas where the limbs had been separated, that the body parts belonged to the same woman whose trunk had been discovered at Pine Apple Gate some six weeks previously.

A Public Inquiry was held at Coldharbour Lane and a special verdict was delivered. 'The two legs found in this parish are those of a female and belong to the trunk of the female lately found in Paddington, in the County of Middlesex, on which a Coroner's Inquest has been held. By whom or how placed here, this jury has no evidence to prove.'

William and Maria Gay lived in Goodge Street, London. William was employed as a broker at Mrs Blanchard's shop at 10 Goodge Street.

On 20 March 1837, a dark thought that had been nagging inside the head of William Gay finally thrust itself forward. Gay applied to Mr Thornton, a churchwarden of the parish of Paddington, for permission to visit the workhouse to inspect the preserved head of the unidentified murdered woman.

The dark thought Gay had been trying his best to suppress, was that the recently discovered body parts may be those of his estranged sister, Hannah Brown, who had left her home on Christmas Eve 1836 and had not been seen or heard of since. Gay and his sister had fallen out about a month before that fateful Christmas Eve and had no longer been on speaking terms.

When Gay first laid eyes upon the disfigured head, encased like a morbid specimen in its glass tomb, his immediate impression was that it may well be that of his sister. The left ear, the eye and the hair, light-coloured mixed with grey, were all familiar to him, though they now took on the appearance of a grotesque caricature.

Gay noticed the left ear was torn at a point where it had been pierced for an earring. He recalled his sister telling him a fellow worker had accidentally torn her ear when pulling on her earring during horseplay. The ear had healed, but the wound had still been perceivable. He told the overseer of the workhouse he was pretty sure it was his sister's head but said he would arrange for his wife to look in and confirm his belief.

Maria Gay duly made her way to the Paddington workhouse to inspect the preserved head. She tried to draw a mental picture of the shape of the face that would have fitted the head, starting from each side of the nose, her sister-in-law's nose having been very flat. She noted the hair was light, intermixed with grey, and the left ear bore the same shape and minor disfigurement as that of her sister-in-law.

Eventually, Mrs Gay confirmed her belief that the head belonged to her sister-in-law, Hannah Brown.

After chasing down so many false leads, the police finally had something concrete to work with and Inspector Feltham began the process of tracking down and speaking to anyone who had recently encountered Hannah Brown.

Brown was described as in her mid-forties. Even her brother could not be sure of her exact age, or of his own for that matter. She was last known to have lodged at 45 Union Street, where she occupied the front kitchen and made a living by washing and mangling laundry. Hannah was said to have been a tall woman with delicate skin, high chested and powerful in appearance, with strong hands befitting someone in her occupation.

During interviews with her friends and neighbours, Inspector Feltham learned Hannah had been about to be married. She had then been due to set off for a new life overseas with her intended, a Mr James Greenacre. Hannah Brown had, however, recently fallen off the grid.

Feltham worked tirelessly, gathering all the background information he could on Hannah Brown and James Greenacre. He eventually received information that there was a gentleman, connected to the family of a former wife of Greenacre, who was aware of the man's present place of residence. Feltham set off immediately to visit the house of the gentleman in question.

As soon as he was informed of the purpose of the Inspector's visit, the man declared, 'Mr Feltham, I will not stand between a murderer and justice.' The man then theatrically threw his cloak over his shoulders and escorted the Inspector to St Alban's Place, where he pointed out the home of James Greenacre.

On the night of 25 March 1837, at about 10:45pm, Feltham knocked on the front door of the property in St Alban's Place. The door was opened by the startled landlord of the house. After Feltham explained why he was calling at such an ungodly hour, the landlord confirmed Greenacre was at home and promptly directed the Inspector to a parlour door, which lay just inside the street door. Feltham knocked on the door and called out 'Greenacre?' The replying voice from within said, 'Yes, what do you want?'

'I want to speak with you, open the door,' the Inspector said.

'Wait a bit while I get the tinder-box and get a light,' came the response. Feltham heard movement inside the room and decided to try the latch of the door, which turned out to be unfastened.

Feltham strode into the darkened room and found James Greenacre standing before him, in the process of putting on a shirt. The Inspector took hold of the man's arm and exclaimed, 'James Greenacre, I have a warrant to take you into custody for the wilful murder of Hannah Brown!'

At this stage, the landlord arrived on the scene carrying a lamp, enabling Feltham to read aloud the full warrant. Feltham then asked, 'Do you know a person of the name of Brown, Hannah Brown?'

'No, I know no Hannah Brown,' Greenacre retorted emphatically.

The unimpressed Inspector pushed for the truth. 'Were you never asked in church to a person of that name?'

'Yes, I was,' Greenacre then meekly admitted.

Greenacre began pulling his stockings on as Feltham continued to question him. 'Where is she now?' he asked.

'I don't know and you have no right to ask me those questions,' Greenacre said indignantly.

'I don't mean to ask you any more questions,' Feltham declared, 'and I caution you as to what you say to me, for, whatever you do say to me, I shall be obliged to repeat elsewhere.'

Feltham noticed the man's trousers were lying on a box by the side of a bed. He told Greenacre to stay where he was before beginning to look through the trouser pockets. It was only then Feltham saw that the men were not alone in the room and that a woman was lying in the bed. 'Who is this woman?' the startled policeman asked.

'Why that is a woman that lives in the room next door and comes to sleep with me,' Greenacre responded.

The woman's name was Sarah Gale.

Feltham told Gale to get up and get dressed. As he was speaking, he heard a rattling sound coming from something the woman was holding in her hand. Asked to hand over whatever she was holding, Gale handed the Inspector a watch and two rings. As the Inspector resumed his search of the man's trousers, Gale slipped out of the bed and began to dress.

Inside the trouser pockets, Feltham found a pinchbeck watch in a leather bag, a purse with one sovereign in it, a cornelian stone and a half-crown in loose change. The cornelian stone bore a crest and the initials J.G. Conducting a search of the room, Feltham found a bunch of eight keys, a spectacle-case and a pencil-case.

After Gale had finished dressing, Feltham asked her what she was carrying in her pockets. The woman emptied her pockets to reveal two pawnbroker's tickets, two cornelian ear-drops set in gold, 2s 5d in change and a set of keys.

One of the pawnbroker's tickets was dated 17 January 1837 and was for two veils, a handkerchief and a pair of shoes. The items had been pawned at Mr Knowles', 19 Bolingbroke Row, Walworth, under the name Mary Stevens. The other ticket was for a pair of shoes that had been pawned for 1s 6d.

A third pawnbrokers' ticket was found in the pocket of a coat hanging behind the parlour door. This ticket was for two silk gowns pawned on the 6 February 1837 for fourteen shillings at Franklin's, late Harrison's, Tottenham Court Road, in the name of William Green.

Having completed his initial search, Feltham sent word for a police coach to be brought to the house. When the coach arrived, the Inspector began ushering Greenacre and Gale towards the door, but the policeman was taken aback when the woman suddenly cried out, 'Oh, there is my child in the next room.'

Feltham checked out the adjacent room, then allowed the woman to fetch and dress the child. As they were waiting, Greenacre asked the Inspector if he could get his great coat out of a nearby corded box. Initially reluctant, Feltham eventually opened the box and handed the coat to the agitated man, who said, 'It is lucky you have come when you did, for I should have been on the quay tomorrow, as I was going off tomorrow morning at 9am.' It then dawned on Feltham that the corded boxes he could see scattered around the room had been prepared for shipment.

When he had finally cleared the room, Feltham locked the doors, pocketed the keys and arranged for Greenacre and Gale to be conveyed directly to the Paddington station-house.

At 6am the following morning, Feltham, accompanied by Sergeant Pegler, returned to Greenacre's lodgings and unlocked four of the corded boxes. The two policemen then began to search for any articles they considered could have at one time belonged to the murdered woman, Hannah Brown. Among the items uncovered was a boa and silk coat, wrapped together in a bundle, and a shawl and white dress.

As the two policemen carried out their meticulous search of the room, they were disturbed by a knock on the door. Pegler quickly ran over and opened the door. Clearly surprised at the sight of the policeman, the man standing outside the door politely inquired if Mr Greenacre was at home. Pegler told the man Greenacre was, in fact, in custody on suspicion of murder and asked the man to identify himself. The man said he was Captain Henry Tanner, of the Mediator, due to sail from St Katherine's Dock for Quebec. A discussion with the Captain revealed the vessel already contained four large chests, placed onboard on the orders of James Greenacre.

Feltham returned to the scene the following day, accompanied by friends and family of the victim. Among the group were Hannah Brown's brother, her sister-in-law and three or four friends who'd been providing the police with information. The Inspector again went through the boxes, this time asking the group to point out any items they believed may have belonged to Hannah.

Among the items of interest found was a bloodstained handkerchief, of the type women of the day wore around their necks. A collar was found laid on a recess, a pair of glasses by the side of the fireplace and a small crepe shawl in the back-room. On the night of his arrest, Greenacre had said the back-room was occupied by Sarah Gale.

The rigorous search also uncovered, in a box which stood by the side of the bed, a pistol and a French knife. Across the box lay a sword-stick and nearby were some bullets which had been very recently and roughly made.

All the items uncovered in the search were removed and taken to the station-house, where they were safely locked away in the evidence room.

In the meantime, Greenacre had not handled his incarceration well and shortly after his arrest he had attempted to kill himself. During the routine half-hourly checks carried out at the Station-house in Paddington, Sergeant Brown had discovered Greenacre lying on the floor of his cell. Greenacre had pushed his foot through a slip knot tied at one end of his neckerchief and had stretched his leg to tighten the noose he had made and placed around his neck at the other end.

The prisoner had shown little sign of life as the policeman had cut the neckerchief then sent for the local parish surgeon, Mr Girdwood. Utilising every method that he knew to try and revive the stricken man, the relieved doctor had eventually heard Greenacre splutter back to life.

James Greenacre was born in 1785, near West Winch, Norfolk. The son of a farmer, Greenacre, unlike his brothers, never acquired a taste for working the land. He did, however, reveal an aptitude for business and his father showed enough faith in the young Greenacre to provide him with the necessary funding to start up a grocery and tea business, based in Woolwich, in 1804.

Shortly after getting the business off the ground, Greenacre married the daughter of Mr Charles Ware, the landlord of the Crown and Anchor in Woolwich, collecting a handsome dowry in the process. Unfortunately, fate was not destined to smile upon the marriage and the young man's wife contracted a horrendous and contagious disease.

Greenacre, against the strong advice of his doctors, attended to the unfortunate young lady throughout her illness until matters reached their inevitable conclusion. As the doctors had feared, Greenacre himself contracted the disease, but he eventually recovered after having endured a life-threatening fever.

The second marriage of James Greenacre was to the daughter of Mr John Romford of Essex. This marriage would be blessed with the birth of seven children, though infant fatalities were commonplace and only two would survive into adulthood. The spectre of early death did not only hover over the children of the time, it haunted adults too. Greenacre's second wife contracted an incurable brain disease and soon followed his first wife to the grave.

Greenacre's third marriage, to the daughter of Mr Simmonds from Long Lane, Bermondsey, would produce two further children.

By the time of this third marriage, Greenacre was a relatively successful and respectable, though strongly opinionated, businessman. He began to build up a property portfolio and acquired properties in Jane Place, Old Kent Road and Bowyer Lane in Camberwell. By the end of the eighteen-twenties, he had moved his expanding grocery business to a much larger shop in the Kent Road.

Greenacre took a keen interest in local politics and was sometimes known to display inflammatory literature in his shop window. One such item was a copy of the King's Speech, deliberately hung upside-down, a fate, he took great delight in telling his customers, he believed it richly deserved.

In 1832, Greenacre was elected parish overseer. This honour was bestowed upon him despite his penchant for annoying his neighbours by practising shooting in the garden behind his house each weekend.

Life seemed to be going rather well for James Greenacre, until, in May 1833, his shop was raided by the excisemen and quantities of sloe leaves, leaves resembling tea leaves and used as an adulterant to tea, were seized. In response, Greenacre wrote a pamphlet about the adulteration of tea and the extent to which it was carried out in and around London. This temporarily helped to increase his custom, until it was made public he, himself, had been caught employing the practice. He was fined £150 by the Board of Excise, an amount he was unable, or unwilling, to pay.

With the impending threat of losing his properties, or heading to debtor's prison, a thoroughly disillusioned Greenacre sold off his interests in several of the properties and departed for America with his youngest son, leaving his wife behind.

The plan had been for Greenacre to send for his wife once he had settled in America. This plan, which he had hoped would protect his interests, was soon thrown into disarray. Within three weeks of his departure, his wife, who had moved to Long Lane to reside with her sister, contracted cholera and died. Their remaining properties in London were claimed by his wife's relatives.

While he was based in America, Greenacre made the acquaintance of a former London coach proprietor. Within a short period of time, he was married to the man's nineteen-year-old daughter.

Greenacre worked as a carpenter but, somewhat more remarkably, during his time in America he invented a type of washing machine for which he managed to obtain a patent. Although the washing machine was never fully developed, it would remain firmly in his thoughts.

In 1835, Greenacre left his latest wife and his son behind and returned to London to sort out his affairs.

On his return, he published an address and letter giving his unique version of the events that had led him to lose everything and forced him to leave for America. Headed, 'To the Humane and Generous Public', the address set out the 'misfortunes, oppressions and mental sufferings of James Greenacre, who was many years a respectable retail grocer in the parish of St George, Southwark, and who, for a trifling infringement of the excise laws, was prevailed upon to flee the country to avoid, as was supposed, a ruinous fine.'

Continuing to describe himself in the third person, Greenacre went on to blame his wife for 'an unfortunate error' in not immediately contacting his creditors. This had resulted in them looking suspiciously on his sudden departure and had consequently forced him into bankruptcy. He then explained how his wife had died shortly after this, quickly followed in death by the solicitor who was managing the affair for the creditors.

Greenacre stated his property had then fallen into the sole possession of his deceased wife's family. They had, he claimed, subsequently cheated the creditors out of their just demands by claiming he had deserted his wife and family and had taken all his property with him to America. He also claimed his property had then been sold for a great deal more than the amount of his debt.

The tale of woe concluded with the following address to the public:-

'James Greenacre begs, therefore, to appeal to a generous public to aid him in obtaining the means to supersede his outlawry and proceed with his case to recover back his property and his two children, whereby he may be enabled to satisfy all his just debts and re-establish himself in business again.'

Greenacre then, generously, added that he would reimburse, when he could, subscriptions from any contributors who made it clear they would like to be repaid by something more tangible than his warmest thanks.

This address to the public, while giving a remarkable insight into the workings of the mind of James Greenacre, paled into insignificance when set against his letter, headed prophetically, 'Horrible Cruelty, Treachery and Cold-Blooded Attempt to Murder.'

Only the words of the man himself could do justice to this particular outpouring:-

'Horrible Cruelty, Treachery and Cold-Blooded Attempt to Murder

Having prepared the annexed address to the humane and generous public in hopes of obtaining the means, by a subscription, to sue for my property, those feelings which modest misfortune can best understand, combined with the feeling of the greatest desire to avoid such an exposure of the wickedness of my cheating relations, who got possession of all my property at the death of my wife and during my absence in America, being anxious to avoid such an exposure I again resolved on sending them a proposal to drop all proceedings, if they would only give me one-tenth part of my property together with my two children.

I sent this proposal to Mr and Mrs Blowen, dealers in fish at Billingsgate; to Mr and Mrs Jones, curriers, York Street, Blackfriars and to John, Thomas and Jane Simmonds, of Carpenter's Place, Camberwell, the childless brothers and sisters of my deceased wife. After waiting three or four days in the hope some arrangement would be acceded to, I called on Mr Blowen, whose wife had got possession of several hundred pounds of my property, for an answer.

Whilst I was calmly addressing myself to him, he called his boy to fetch 'the thing', as he called it, a large bludgeon made of whalebone and lead. With this, he put himself in an attitude to assault me. I, however, continued to argue the proprietary of an arrangement; and the justness and moderation of my claim, in a tone and manner that seemed to soften his savage breast; and induced him to propose for me to call on him on the Monday (this being Saturday) when he proposed to see the remainder of the family on the subject (all of whom have shared in the spoils of my property). To my great surprise he, on my leaving, tendered me his hand to shake.

I looked on this as a favourable omen, little suspecting Mr Blowen was mediating such cold-blooded cowardice as to induce me to call on Monday to murder me. He obviously suspected I had been prepared to defend myself; which indeed I had, and it is well for him he did not use his bludgeon.

I returned to my lodging to wait till Monday, fully

confident an arrangement would be made, as I felt determined to facilitate that arrangement, by acceding to their own terms, if at all reasonable. With this determination to settle the affair at my own expense and hindrance, I wrote to each of those gentlemen who kindly offered to aid me in getting up a subscription, to thank them for their kindness, expressing the great pleasure I felt in being able to inform them I was likely to settle the affair amicably.

Such were my sanguine opinions and dependence upon Mr Blowen's pretend friendship, which induced me to call at his house on the Monday, unprepared for an assault and unsuspecting of danger.

The door was opened by the same boy who attended to Blowen on the Saturday. I first met my daughter in the passage, who saluted me I believe with becoming sentiment and not like the kiss of Judas or Blowen's shake of the hand. This perfect prototype of Judas next presented himself and considering he had tendered me his hand on parting, I could not do less than offer him wine on our meeting but which, however, he refused.

The following conversation and scene now took place.

'Well, what do you want?' Blowen said, in the most insolent tone and gesture.

'Why,' I said, 'I have called by your appointment to know the determination of yourself and the rest of the family about them restoring to me some part of my property, with my two children.'

'Your children you may have, but your property we know nothing about.'

'Well, let me ask my daughter Sarah what became of the things that were in her mother's possession when she died. You know I left plenty of beds and every requisite for our use to last us for many years to come and more than one thousand pounds in value, all of which had been the result of my own industry.'

'You shall not ask her any questions here. You may go and prove what you can by law.'

At this point my daughter came downstairs and whilst my eyes were directed towards her, to ask her a question, this cowardly ruffian drew from under his coat his bludgeon, loaded at the end with a lump of lead, with which he struck me violently on the back of my head.

It was now evident his intentions were to murder me. His making of this unprovoked attack, the violent manner of expressing himself, the injustice of his few remarks, the wild agitation of his features and the concealment of other male branches of the family in an adjoining room, all combined to show this was a premeditated plot to take my life, which was only prevented by the cry of murder and the providential circumstances of a policeman, 88 of M Division, happening to be passing the door at the moment of attack.

The boy had been ordered from the scene to fetch a policeman, it being intended to dispatch me in the meantime and the defence of justifiable homicide would no doubt have been successfully set up by such a host of honest and able swearers. The plot failed through the prompt attendance of this officer, who was afterwards grossly insulted for applying to know the nature of the charge. The fact is, he was not wanted to lead me away and he disappointed them by coming too soon to carry me off. The door was, therefore, slammed in his face.

I only got a sight of one of the other men, the same who fetched about three hundred pounds worth of my property from the Docks, which I had placed there ready to come along with my wife to America, which property is denied, as is all the rest, notwithstanding I can prove the day and hour they were had from the Docks, the cart that was employed, as also the expense that was paid for warehouse rent and every particular of this and my other property, which is explained in the book to be given to every subscriber who will generously assist me in obtaining the means of recovering my property.

I do hereby solemnly pledge my word it shall be my first and chief pleasure to refund the subscription of every person who will aid me to sue for my property, who will advance his raise to be returned; for which purpose the books are double-ruled with lines, headed 'free donations' and 'donations to be refunded.'

My oppressors know my proofs against them are clear and indefeasible and if I meet with supporters to supersede my outlawry, I am sure to recover my property. Knowing this, they are now anxious to destroy me, lest the voice of truth should be heard and sympathy and justice prevail.

Any lady or gentleman who will aid the cause of the oppressed, by giving the reference of one or more of their humane and kind-hearted acquaintances that they may be called upon, such kindness will aid the cause of justice and will meet with the strictest honour and indelible attitude of JAMES GREENACRE.'

The letter was accompanied by a caution (as if one was needed):-

'Caution: Being now aware a design is intended upon my life, I would caution my cheating enemies, for their own sakes, that I shall always be prepared with the means of defence.

I trust the generous public will enable me to set aside the outlawry (which my enemies were the cause of) so I may have the protection of the law and not be robbed, maimed and murdered with impunity.'

At least Greenacre's concerns go some way to explaining the array of weapons Inspector Feltham discover on the box next to the bed in St Alban's Place.

By 1836, Greenacre was residing at 6 Carpenter's Buildings, Camberwell, with his lover, Sarah Gale. It was while living there he became the subject of several disturbing allegations.

On 31 May of that year, Greenacre was moved to attend Union Hall to obtain a warrant against Mr and Mrs Gill of Bowyer Lane, Camberwell. The couple had accused him of having murdered an illegitimate child, alleged to have been born through his relationship with Gale. The child, who had gone missing, was alleged to have been left on the steps of a nearby workhouse by Greenacre and Gale and was thought to have died soon after.

As rumours of a child murder spread through the neighbourhood, an angry mob assembled in front of Greenacre's house and threatened to 'get him hanged'. When the case was brought before Magistrates, the accusations were found to be without foundation and Mr and Mrs Gill were held on charges of 'using language of a threatening and unfounded description'.

Greenacre was later accused of drugging a woman and forcing her into having an abortion, but this charge was subsequently withdrawn for lack of evidence.

As his troubled year of 1836 was drawing to a close, James Greenacre finally had some good news to announce, he was due to be married in St Giles Church, on Christmas Day, to washer-woman Hannah Brown.

During their courtship, Hannah Brown had told James Grenache that she had managed to save a considerable sum of money, around four hundred pounds. Greenacre suggested to Hannah that she should give up work, sell-off her mangle and furniture and keep the proceeds for pocket money. He let it be known he owned considerable property himself and was in no need of any share of the proceeds from the sale.

With the wedding date set for Christmas Day, Hannah and her husband-to-be visited her friends, Hannah Davis and her husband Evan, to inform them of the impending happy event.

After offering their sincere congratulations, Mr and Mrs Davis suggested hosting the couple's wedding dinner at their house in Bartholomew Close, a proposal which Brown and Greenacre were more than happy to accept.

Towards the end of the evening, Greenacre asked Mr Davis if he would be prepared to take on the duty of giving away the bride and if he would allow his daughter to be a bridesmaid. Davis readily agreed and arrangements were made for them all to meet up at the Angel Pub, near St Giles Church, on the day of the ceremony.

It came as a huge surprise, therefore, when, on the eve of the wedding, Hannah Davis opened her front door to find a very agitated James Greenacre standing before her. Greenacre, who was carrying a tightly wrapped bundle under his arm, asked the woman if she had seen Hannah Brown recently, or was aware of her whereabouts. Mrs Davis told Greenacre she had not seen Hannah and had still been expecting to meet the couple the following day for their wedding ceremony.

Greenacre explained that he and Hannah had fallen out.

He claimed Hannah had deceived him by lying about the value of the property which she had told him she possessed. After the argument, Hannah had stormed out of the house and declared the wedding was off.

Several days passed and Hannah Davis had still heard nothing from Hannah Brown. Surprised and confused by the way things had developed, Mrs Davis tried to convince herself Hannah had probably felt foolish at the sudden break-up and had been too ashamed to show face. It would be many days later that her thoughts would turn to what may have been wrapped up in the bundle James Greenacre had been carrying under his arm when he had appeared at her door on the eve of his wedding.

On 27 December 1836, Greenacre called at a broker's shop at 10 Goodge Street. The owner of the shop, Mrs Blanchard, had been a close friend of Hannah Brown's since childhood and Greenacre stopped by to enquire whether the woman had recently seen or heard from Hannah.

Mrs Blanchard invited Greenacre into the shop to talk, but he excused himself, saying he was in a somewhat of a hurry. Instead, he had a brief discussion with the woman at the front door.

Greenacre said Hannah had let him down badly, claiming to have discovered she had attempted to obtain goods at a tally-shop in his name and had lied about having property of her own. Warming to the subject, Greenacre then told the open-mouthed Mrs Blanchard that he had heard, from people he knew, that Hannah had been thinking about taking on a shop in London instead of going overseas with him. He continued his rant by explaining to the dumbstruck woman how his marrying Hannah would have plunged him into a state of misery and ruin.

It was at this stage a man appeared on the scene from the kitchen below. A relieved Mrs Blanchard took the opportunity to introduce the man to Greenacre. The man was introduced as William Gay, brother of Hannah Brown. The colour quickly drained from Greenacre's face and he hurriedly shook the man's hand, before muttering a hasty 'good evening' and scurrying off down the road.

This bizarre event was the first-time William Gay had even heard of James Greenacre. Gay said to Mrs Blanchard he did not believe his sister, with whom he had fallen out several months earlier, would have told Greenacre about him. Gay believed the meeting of the two men, which had so visibly shaken Greenacre, to have been an extraordinary coincidence.

On Monday 27 March 1837, the excitement spreading throughout the Paddington and Marylebone parishes of London was palpable. The crowds were aware a man and woman had been apprehended in connection with the mutilated remains discovered scattered around the area. Now, they were gathering to see the pair being brought before the Bench at the Marylebone Office.

Around 5,000 people had congregated around the Office by the time Inspector Feltham delivered the prisoners. To avoid the mob, Greenacre and Gale were smuggled in through the Magistrate's door in High Street. A gaunt looking James Greenacre, still clearly suffering the effects of his failed suicide bid, was dressed in the great coat Feltham had allowed him to take during his arrest. After a brief glance around the room, he settled, placing his elbow on the metal railing before him and resting his cheek upon his left hand. Sarah Gale was modestly dressed and sat, with her young child by her side, trying to take in all that was happening in the vast room.

Mr Rawlinson, the sitting Magistrate for the day, led the Inquiry. He began by having Constable Pegler recount his story of the discovery of the woman's torso in the sack found at Pine Apple Gate.

Pegler then went on to reveal that, after the prisoners had been arrested, he had gone with Inspector Feltham to carry out a search of the property at St Alban's Place. During the search, he had discovered a light-coloured infant's frock. Based on the material from which the frock had been fashioned and the nankeen patches on the front it, Pegler was of the view the frock was from the same source material as the blood-soaked rags discovered beside the sack at Pine Apple Gate.

Elizabeth Corney, the wife of shoemaker John Corney, was called next. The Corney's place of residence was 46 Union Street and they also owned the property next door, which they had leased to Hannah Brown. Mrs Corney recalled a conversation she'd had with Hannah during which her tenant had informed her she was soon to be married and was planning to move abroad. Corney had witnessed Hannah selling off all her furniture, as well as the mangle from which she had made her living. She had seen Hannah's husband-to-be on a couple of occasions during the house clearance, but could not swear to the Court that the man she had seen was James Greenacre.

When Hannah's lease had drawn to an end, she had asked Corney for permission to hang onto the keys of the property for a couple of extra days, claiming she had left behind a few items she intended to collect later. Elizabeth Corney would never set eyes upon Hannah Brown again.

As time passed, Corney concluded that Hannah was not

going to return and she and her husband forced entry to the property. All that had been left behind was an empty birdcage.

Hannah and Evan Davis were next up. They told the tale of Greenacre and Brown's marriage arrangements and Greenacre's subsequent surprise appearance at their door to inform them the wedding had been called off.

William Gay, Hannah Brown's brother, then testified and provided details of his strained relationship with his sister and of his bizarre first meeting with James Greenacre at the broker's shop in Goodge Street.

Inspector Feltham was called to provide an account of his arrest of James Greenacre and Sarah Gale and the subsequent search of their premises. The Inspector went on to say that Hannah Davis had identified earrings found during the search as being identical to ones she had seen being worn by Hannah Brown. Other witnesses had identified a watch and some silk dresses as being very much like those that had belonged to Brown.

At this point, Mr Rawlinson arranged for Gale to be removed from the room and he then addressed Greenacre directly. He advised Greenacre that he was about to have him remanded for re-examination. Rawlinson then offered Greenacre the opportunity to make a statement, if he so wished, that would be taken down by the clerk.

This was an opportunity that a man such as Greenacre could not resist. He rose to his feet and in a clear and confident voice made the following statement:-

'I have to state that in the evidence given there are many direct falsehoods. I distinctly told Mrs Davis we had no words of any consequence, that is, no quarrel. What I mentioned to her was that I had found out Mrs Brown had no money at all and had tried to set up things, in my name, at a tally shop. I merely argued the point with her, but there had been no dispute worth speaking of.

There may have been duplicity on both sides. I represented myself to her as a man of property and I found out she was not a suitable companion for me, which may fairly be concluded from her conduct towards her brothers and sisters.

I'll adhere strictly to the truth in what I am saying, although there are many circumstances in the evidence combining against me and which may, perhaps, cost me my life.

One of the witnesses has said I helped to move the boxes on the Saturday. That is true, but I will precede that remark by stating I had this female (the other prisoner) in a room at the time, where she was lodging and doing my cooking for me. I gave her notice to leave before Mrs Brown coming home and she had left accordingly.

On the Saturday night before Christmas Day, Mrs Brown came down to my house, rather fresh from drinking having during the morning treated the coachman, and insisted on having more rum, a quantity of which she had with her tea. I then thought it a favourable opportunity to press upon her for the state of her circumstances. She was very reluctant to give me any answer and I told her she had very often dropped insinuations into my hearing about having property enough to go into business and she had said she could command, at any time, three or four hundred pounds.

I told her I had made some inquiry about her character and had ascertained she had been to Smith's tally shop, in Longacre, and had tried to procure silk gowns in my name. She put on a feigned laugh and retaliated by saying she thought I had been deceiving her regarding my property, by misrepresenting it.

During this conversation, she was reeling backwards and forwards in her chair, which was on the swing, and, as I am determined to adhere strictly to the truth, I must say that I put my foot against the chair and she fell back, with great violence, against a block of wood I had been using. This alarmed me very much and I went around the table and took her by the hand and kept shaking her, but she appeared to be completely gone.

It is impossible to give an accurate description of my feelings at the time and, in the state of excitement I was in, I unfortunately determined on putting her away. I deliberated for a little while and then made up my mind to conceal her death in the manner already gone forth to the world. I thought it might be safer that way than if I gave an account of what had occurred.

No one individual, up to the present moment, had the least knowledge of what I have stated here. This female, Sarah Gale, I perfectly exonerate from having any more knowledge of it than any other person, as she was away from the house. Some days after, when I had put away the body, I called on this woman and solicited her to return to the apartment. As to the trunks and other things, I told this female that as Mrs Brown had left them here, we would pledge all we could. The whole of the articles pawned fetched only three pounds.

That's all I wish to say. Mrs Brown had eleven sovereigns by her and a few shillings in silver and that is a true statement of the facts.'

As the gasping gallery took in the full implications of the

statement, Mr Rawlinson put it to Greenacre that it had been sworn that on Christmas Eve, he had been located in Bartholomew Close.

'We had tea, me and Mrs Brown,' Greenacre replied, 'and it was on the same night her death occurred that I called on Mrs Davis, to stop them going to the church. There was no quarrel between me and the deceased.'

After Greenacre's statement, Gale was brought back before the Bench. Mr Rawlinson offered her the opportunity to make a statement before she would be committed for re-examination.

'I know nothing about it, I was not at Camberwell,' Gale said.

Greenacre quickly interjected, exclaiming, 'She knows nothing about it whatever!'

Gale continued. 'These rings taken from me are mine. The one I gave five shillings and sixpence for in the City twelve months ago and the other my little boy found, together with a half-sovereign, two half-crowns and sixpence in copper, whilst digging in the garden. The ear drops I've had for seven or eight years and with respect to the shoes, a Mrs Andrews gave me one of the tickets and the other I picked up on the street near my own house.'

'Mr Greenacre told me to leave his house a fortnight before Christmas, but I did not leave then as I could not suit myself with lodgings. I went away on the following Thursday. On the Monday week after that, I returned to the house and he told me the correspondence between him and Mrs Brown was broken off. That's all I have to say.'

With that, Greenacre and Gale were ordered to be brought up again on the following Saturday.

As the prisoners were led away, the enthralled crowds, the largest that had ever collected around the Marylebone Office, dispersed to discuss the sensational events of the day.

On Saturday, 1 April 1837, the Inquiry into the death of Hannah Brown was due to resume. A large, hostile, crowd had gathered in the streets surrounding the Marylebone Office. In anticipation of this, the prisoners had been conveyed to the Office in the early hours of the morning in two coaches, rather than the usual highly visible Prison Van.

Despite the precautions, the prisoners still had to be hustled through a multitude of early-risers, who had already gathered outside the Office in the hope of getting a better look at the accused. Greenacre and Gale were eventually brought into the building through the Magistrate's private door.

Large numbers of well-dressed women were dotted around the gallery, together with many distinguished parish residents and numerous members of the press when the Inquiry resumed at 11am.

Matthias Ralph was called as the first witness and recounted his story of the finding of the woman's head in the lock-gate on the Regent's Canal. Ralph's testimony was followed by that of James Page, the man who discovered the legs and thighs.

Mr Girdwood, the surgeon, was next and he went over the evidence he had previously provided at the Paddington Inquest, regarding his examination of the mutilated remains of the female.

Susanne Dillon, the current resident in the property at 6 Carpenter's Buildings, Camberwell, where Greenacre had lived, was next up. Dillon and her husband John had lived in the property for a period of eight weeks and Greenacre was their landlord.

Dillon confirmed she had known both Greenacre and Gale and had been aware they had been residing, as a couple, in the property during the period covering the Christmas of 1836. Her recollection was that Gale had moved into the property around the October of that year. She was not aware of Greenacre's family arrangements before that time.

When pressed on whether she had been aware of anything of note having happened at the house over the Christmas period, Dillon recalled having seen Gale on Boxing Day, at about 7pm. The woman had been trying to placate her child, who was screaming violently.

The Boxing Day incident was backed up by the next witness, Henrietta Edmonds, Greenacre's next-door neighbour at 5 Carpenter's Buildings. Edmonds had noticed the shutters of the property at number 6 had been closed for three or four full days over the Christmas week, which she had considered unusual, as the house was still occupied.

Some three weeks later, Edmonds, accompanied by Susanne Dillon, had gone to look at the property at number 6, which had been put up for let. The two women had been greeted at the door by Sarah Gale, who'd had her little boy by her side. The women had noticed the chimney in the front parlour was boarded up and the room had emitted a strong smell as if it had been fumigated with brimstone.

Frances Andrews, the wife of a local shoemaker and another resident of Carpenter's Buildings, was then called. Andrews, who was visibly distressed, revealed she had known both Greenacre and Gale since around May 1836. She had become aware that Gale was struggling financially and had noted the woman and her little boy were looking somewhat malnourished. Andrews had arranged for Gale to obtain some shoe-binding work and had become a frequent visitor to the property at number 6.

Mrs Andrews said she'd had no knowledge of Greenacre and Gale having any plans to be married but had been told by the couple they were soon to have a visitor staying with them for a few days. On 18 December 1836, Andrews had seen a darkish looking woman, dressed in a pea green gown with a collar over the shoulder, a black veil and a silk bonnet, arrive at number 6. Later that same day, the eagle-eyed Mrs Andrews had seen Greenacre and the mystery woman standing at the gate of the property, looking at some of the plants in the garden. She had never seen the woman again after that day.

On the Christmas Eve of 1836, Gale had turned up at Mrs Andrews' house with an empty kettle and had asked her if she would be able to provide some water. Andrews, unfortunately, had not been able to do so. On Boxing Day, Andrews had gone to Gale's house to hand over some plum pudding for the little boy. At that time, Gale gave every appearance of still being an inmate of the house and Mrs Andrews found everything to be as normal.

Andrews had noticed the shutters of the house had been closed on Christmas Day and had assumed Greenacre and Gale had been out, otherwise, as she had said to Gale at the time, she would have delivered the plum pudding on Christmas Day. Gale had informed her she'd been home on Christmas Day, but Greenacre had gone out to dinner in Monmouth Street, a Christmas arrangement that struck Andrews as odd at the time.

Mrs Andrews next visited the property on 28 December, to hand in some water, and found the door was locked. She knocked on the door, which was opened by Greenacre, who invited her in for a quick Christmas drink. Mrs Andrews returned home and, later that same morning, Gale appeared at her door and asked her if she could look after the little boy, who was carrying a bacon sandwich wrapped in a handkerchief, for a short time. Gale did not return to collect the boy over the next few days.

The next witness to be called was pawnbroker Joseph Knowles. Knowles produced for the Inquiry a pair of shoes, a woman's neckerchief, a white veil and a black veil. He then stated that, without a doubt, the items had been pledged by the female prisoner on 17 January 1837, under the name Mary Stevens of 9 East Lane.

Knowles had advanced the amount requested on the items, two pounds. The items had been wrapped in a handkerchief, which Knowles had only later noticed was blood-stained. The handkerchief was then passed to the Magistrate for examination.

Hannah Davis then spoke again and confirmed she believed the shoes and veils to have previously belonged to Hannah Brown. Mrs Davis then went on to identify several of the items removed from the properties in Carpenter's Buildings and St Alban's Place by Inspector Feltham.

Mrs Davis' daughter, who had been due to be a bridesmaid at the wedding of Greenacre and Hannah Brown, was then called and the young girl identified a shawl, a collar, a boa, a cloak and a white veil she believed she had previously seen in the possession of Hannah Brown.

Next up was Rebecca Smith, the sister of Hannah Brown. Mrs Smith identified several items that had been recovered by Inspector Feltham as having previously belonged to her sister, particularly, a trunk and a card-box.

A couple of further witnesses were called to identify items believed to have been owned by Hannah Brown, before the inquiry heard from Thomas Chisholm, a shoemaker from Pitt Street, Camberwell.

Chisholm recounted how, a week after Christmas 1836, he had been heading home from work, walking down Bowyer Lane, when he had been tapped on the shoulder by a stranger. The man had asked him if he'd be interested in a job and had then told him he required assistance to move some goods. Chisholm, keen to earn an extra few bob, had followed the man up Windmill Lane. As they neared the top of the road, the man had asked a boy, who'd been walking nearby, if he would also be willing to assist in moving the goods. The boy readily agreed and the three of them headed up to Carpenter's Place, where they came upon a stationed hand-truck.

Several boxes had been stacked outside the door of Greenacre's property and the two men and the boy began the job of loading them onto the hand-truck. They then loaded a bed, bedstead, two chairs and various other items. Greenacre tied down the items with a cord before declaring, 'Now all's done and I am going to leave the country.'

Chisholm recalled Sarah Gale had then appeared from within the property, dressed in a plaid cloak. Chisholm claimed to have overheard her say to Greenacre that he had 'done for himself'. Greenacre, with the assistance of Chisholm and the boy, pulled the truck until they arrived in Elephant and Castle. It was then Chisholm noticed Gale was no longer with them. She had quietly slipped away without a word to anyone.

Greenacre told Chisholm he was going to unload some of the furniture and deliver it to a broker who had offered to buy it. After some haggling, he eventually paid sixpence to Chisholm and threepence to the boy. He then took charge of the hand-truck, which he said he was planning to return after he had conveyed all the boxes to the dock.

Following Chisholm's testimony, the Magistrate asked if there were any further witnesses to be called. On hearing there were not, he addressed Greenacre directly, informing him that due to the volume of the depositions, he would be remanded until Wednesday next, when all the evidence given to date would be read over.

Rawlinson then asked the two prisoners if they wished to make a statement. Gale declined the offer but Greenacre, against the advice of his counsel, chose to speak.

'Ever since I have been incarcerated in prison, I have not even been permitted to look at a newspaper,' Greenacre said, 'but, from the information I have received, I believe it is currently reported that a child was murdered by me. This story was trumped up out of malice and spite and emanated from Carpenter's Place.'

'The facts of the case are these,' Greenacre claimed, 'a young woman, a lodger of mine, was suddenly seized with the pain of labour when her groans brought me to her door. I went in and the woman, before any professional help could arrive, had given birth to a child. I was present at the delivery and I think I may state, without fear of contradiction, that to me she owes her life.'

'The infant was, soon after its birth, removed from my house,' Greenacre went on, 'to the residence of one of the female's friends, but I know not now where it is. If it is dead, I can solemnly swear I had no hand in it and it's a very hard case that I should be pointed at as the murderer.'

Greenacre was then asked by the Magistrate if he had

anything he wished to say that was pertinent to the charge against him.

'Nothing more than this. The occurrence was purely an accident, but, unhappily, as melancholy and unfortunate a one as ever befell a man. But that the death was caused by accident is true and I shall ever regret I omitted to disclose the real facts of the case.'

As the prisoners were being led out, Hannah Brown's sister was moved to tears and cried out, 'Oh my poor sister, my dear, dear sister,' before being helped into the passageway by two police officers.

Greenacre and Gale were conveyed from the Inquiry in two separate coaches at around 5pm. They had to make their way through a crowd that had grown even more hostile over the course of the day. The police were required to demonstrate considerable restraint as they protected the prisoners from the mob, while the coaches made their painfully slow journey from the Marylebone Office to the respective prisons.

It would be well after 6pm before some semblance of order was restored to the streets and the crowds began to disperse.

As he sat alone in his cell, contemplating his fate, Greenacre decided it would be a good idea to pen a letter attacking the coverage he had received from the press. He then, somehow, managed to smuggle the letter out to one of the targets of his ire, a newspaper reporter. The plan must have made sense to the man at the time.

The letter read:-

'To a Humane and Enlightened Public.

Everything ingenuity and malice could invent to influence the minds of the ignorant and to fill the minds of the good and religious with awe, has been the result of newspaper comment against me.

It is said the finger of God is manifest to bringing this horrid and wilful murder to light, only the day before my flight to America. I contend this manifestation of Divine Providence is to serve my case or the cause of a suffering mind to prevent me from a life of continual dread of being fetched back from America upon this awful charge, which would certainly have been the result if the deceased had not been recognised until I had departed.

Thus, it may be shown Providence is on my side. Again, if in my crossing the Atlantic, or by any other means, my death had ensued, the fatal conviction of an innocent female would certainly have been the result. Suspicion would have been too strong to have saved her. It was for God and God alone to prevent this fatal termination. No human mind could have discerned anything in her favour if my death had preceded this investigation.

God is just and God should be praised for this timely interference to prevent my premature death through either my crossing the sea, or the distracted state of my mind. I hope, therefore, my unfortunate situation may not be prejudiced by malice and perverted comments.

I trust other papers will copy this address.

James Greenacre.'

The publication of the letter served to add even greater numbers to the crowds that gathered in the streets leading to the Marylebone Office for the resumption of the Inquiry, on 5 April 1837.

If the intention of Greenacre's letter had been to win some form of support from the public, he had badly misjudged their sense of humanity and enlightenment regarding his plight. The crowd were distinctly hostile and were baying for blood as the hour approached when the coaches were expected to bring the two prisoners from their respective jails. The mob was to be disappointed.

In anticipation of a repeat of the previous chaotic scenes in Marylebone, Mr Rawlinson had the previous evening, decided to continue the Inquiry within the New Prison, in Clerkenwell, where Greenacre was being held. Gale was to be brought there from the House of Corrections. The witnesses, accompanied by Inspector Feltham, were conveyed to the new site and were accommodated in a private room within the New Prison.

Although the change of venue had thrown off the hostile crowds gathering at Marylebone, hundreds of people had already gathered outside the New Prison in expectation of seeing Greenacre leaving from there. They were soon joined by a group that had followed the carriage bringing Gale from the House of Corrections.

New venue, same hysteria.

A trembling Gale, looking even paler and more distressed than she had during her earlier appearances, held her child by the hand and sat separated from a dejected looking Greenacre as proceedings resumed.

Mr Fell, the Chief Clerk, was asked by Rawlinson to read over all the evidence that had been given during the first two examinations. As Fell reached the part of the evidence provided by Mrs Davis, regarding the marriage arrangements, Greenacre became visibly agitated before fixing his gaze upon Davis, who was situated close to where Sarah Gale was positioned.

Fell continued to read the evidence, but when he reached the part concerning Inspector Feltham's testimony on the finding of the boxes, Greenacre asked if he might be permitted to speak. He was told by Mr Rawlinson that he would be required to wait until the reading was concluded.

After he had finished reading the evidence, Mr Fell was asked to read out the statement Greenacre had made at the earlier hearing. Rawlinson then asked Greenacre if he had anything further to say and if he would now be prepared to sign that statement. Greenacre confirmed he had nothing further to add and duly signed the statement.

Gale was then read her own statement, in which she had claimed she had not been present in Camberwell at the time of the alleged murder. After stating she wished to say nothing further, she too agreed to sign her statement. As she walked forward with faltering steps to apply her signature, Greenacre urged the trembling woman, 'Sign, sign. Don't frighten yourself at what people say about you're going to be hung and all that stuff.' Most reassuring.

The reading of the evidence and the signatures of the statements had taken well over an hour and Rawlinson asked the defence if they wished to have the Inquiry postponed until the next sessions, in the hope the excitement surrounding the case may have subsided by then. Mr Price, who was representing the prisoners, replied that they were anxious there should be no further delay and offered the opinion that a postponement would be more likely to increase the excitement surrounding the case than lessen it.

After discussions between the Bench, the defence and the prosecution, it was decided the case should go before a jury at the earliest opportunity. The prisoners were committed to stand trial for the murder of Hannah Brown.

On Monday 10 April 1837, the trial of James Greenacre, for the wilful murder of Hannah Brown, and Sarah Gale, for feloniously aiding, assisting and counselling in the said murder, began at the Old Bailey.

It almost goes without saying that the streets around the courthouse were packed. In fact, the numbers rivalled those that would have been drawn to witness a public execution at the time. The efforts to obtain access to the courtroom were intense and police were on hand to ensure the successful applicants could make their way through the crowds. They had, after all, paid a sovereign each for the privilege.

As the two prisoners were led into the room, a well-dressed Greenacre surveyed the scene before him, while Gale walked, in faltering steps, with her head bowed down.

Mr Adolphus, Mr Clarkson and Mr Bodkin appeared for the prosecution on behalf of the parish of Paddington. Mr Price and Mr Payne appeared for the defendants, before Lord Chief Justice Tindal.

Adolphus was first to rise and he outlined for the jury their responsibilities, before laying out the facts of the case as they were perceived by the prosecution. Adolphus began by reading out Greenacre's own statement regarding the circumstances of the death of Hannah Brown. He then pointed out that the evidence of the surgeon who had examined the body was at variance with Greenacre's assertion that Hannah had consumed a quantity of rum on the night of her death. Indeed, no evidence of the consumption of rum or any other spirits could be found, except for of a small trace of gin.

Next, Adolphus attacked Greenacre's claim that Hannah

had fallen from her chair and struck her head on a block of wood, causing a fracture to the back of the head. The barrister pointed out this was also contradicted by the medical witnesses, who would testify that death had been caused by a blow to the front of the head which had caused the eye of the deceased to become dislodged. The surgeon would also testify as to how the woman's throat must have then been cut, which would account for the complete exhaustion of blood from the head and body.

The prosecutor then pointed to the fact Greenacre's house had been closed up over the period immediately following the death of Hannah Brown. He next stated that the sack in which the body had been found had gone missing from the premises of a cabinet maker, Mr Ward, and Greenacre had been a visitor at the premises just a day or two before the sack had gone missing.

Adolphus then turned his attention to Elizabeth Gale and the fact she had returned to Greenacre on the very day Hannah had left her own home to go there. He was of the belief that the size of the room in which the murder was presumed to have been committed precluded any possibility of it having been concealed from Gale. The fact a portion of the property of the victim had been in Gale's possession at the time of her arrest would also go to strengthen the impression she had played a key role in the covering up of the murder.

Following his opening statement, Adolphus produced the various witnesses required to back up his assertions. The witnesses that had testified at the initial Inquiry into the death of Hannah Brown were all called again to outline the case for the prosecution.

The first day's proceedings lasted until 8pm, when the

Judge informed the jury they would be accommodated in the London Coffeehouse, in Ludgate Hill, under the charge of the sheriff's assistant, Mr Hemp, until the resumption of the trial the following day.

On the second day of the trial, before another packed public gallery, the prosecution continued to put their case. A well-presented Greenacre again sat looking impassive, whilst Gale looked as if the stress was taking its toll.

Included in the evidence presented on day two of the trial were the signed statements made by the defendants during the Inquiry.

Before surgeon John Birtwhistle was sworn in, to provide evidence as to cause of death and the draining of the victim's blood, it was agreed that the females in the gallery would be temporarily removed due to the graphic nature of the evidence. Birtwhistle then spoke as to the blows he believed had been received by Hannah Brown, the cutting-up of the body and the contents found in the victim's stomach.

The prosecution case was concluded at 3pm on the second day of the trial and the case for the defence began at 3:25 that same day.

The Judge, firstly, declared that in line with an application made to the Court earlier in the proceedings, all property that had not been identified as having belonged to the deceased would be returned to the prisoners at the end of the trial. Mr Price then rose to address the jury on behalf of the defence.

Price began by opining that there were difficulties in this case which he believed had never been presented in a Court of Justice before. He clarified that the most important difficulties connected with the defence were those presented by Greenacre himself. Although Mr Price believed he would not be able to provide the jury with an acceptable excuse for Greenacre's actions following the death of Hannah Brown, he hoped to at least provide some extraordinary extenuating circumstances.

The barrister informed the jury of his belief that Greenacre had been as shocked by the recollections of his own actions as any member of the jury or the public could possibly have been. He was sure that from the moment the prisoner had recovered his senses, he had bitterly regretted his offences against decency and respect for the dead. Price then claimed Greenacre was sorry that, even at the risk to his own life, he had not surrendered himself immediately, rather than carrying with him the dreadful misery the recollections of his actions had brought.

Another difficulty in the case, Price ventured, had been caused by the behemoth that was the press. He was of the view the newspapers had set out to crush the prisoner, to scatter his friends and relations and in turn to paralyse his advocate. He continued his withering attack on the press by comparing them with the machine that had, in a former time, been used to physically press men to death in Newgate Prison.

Price claimed that every witness called to date, despite their best efforts, had in some way been prejudiced by a portion of the newspaper press.

Moving on, Price declared to the jury that he wished they could hear the prisoners make their own defence, because, in the case of Sarah Gale, they would have heard the language of truth from the lips of innocence. He held this view because he had heard it himself and was in no doubt Gale was not guilty of the charges brought against her.

The barrister then drew the jury's attention to a third

prisoner entangled in this case, a young and innocent child who at this very time was, perhaps, playing in the grounds of Newgate Prison, blissfully unaware of the events unfolding in the courtroom. Price asserted that Sarah Gale was every bit as innocent as her little child.

Price then put to the jury that however repulsed they may have been by the hideous treatment of the body of the deceased, they should not allow this to cloud their judgement as to whether death had been caused by a horrific accident, rather than a cold-blooded murder. He believed the actions Greenacre had taken following the death of Hannah Brown could only be the result of a fevered brain, haunted by the frantic fury of a frenzied imagination as he looked upon the prone body of the woman he had planned to marry. He then asked the jury to consider if they really believed any man in his calm, cool senses, whatever the danger he may be exposing himself to, could have suggested to his mind so cruel a means of concealment. Nothing but a temporary insanity, Price concluded, could have sustained a man through the performance of such an atrocious operation.

The lawyer then reminded the jury Greenacre had admitted to his actions in a candid confession. In doing so, he had relieved them from many difficulties. Having done this, Price believed the man was entitled to claim some favourable consideration. Indeed, Price pointed out, it had come as a surprise to the defence that the prosecution had taken two days to prove what had already been fully and fairly admitted by the prisoner himself.

The prisoner had admitted his connection to the woman, his being with her at the time of death and his having her clothes in his possession. It had appeared to Price that the prosecution would only have been content with a confession of murder. He contended that if any one part of the statement of the prisoner was to be considered, then the prosecution ought to take the rest with it. The full confession showed the conduct of the prisoner did not amount to the crime of murder.

Even if the confession was not taken as being entirely correct and a scenario had played out where words had occurred between the two, resulting in Greenacre having, under some perceived provocation, risen from his seat, striking the woman dead, Price contended this would likely result in the Judge steering the jury towards a verdict of manslaughter.

The only evidence submitted by the prosecution that could be construed as alluding to premeditation, Price claimed, was the mute sack that had been exhibited to the jury. There was nothing else that could give the impression a murder had been planned. Right up until the time of death, the prisoner and the deceased had been on cordial terms. They were about to be married, a date had been set and arrangements had been made with friends of the deceased who were to entertain them on their wedding day.

Price put to the jury that the prosecution had not made a case that would allow them to deliver a verdict of premeditated murder. There was no motive, no evidence of malice and not even a single word of an angry nature had been proved. Any property the victim had, however great or small, would have come under the control of the accused by marriage, so he had no incentive to acquire it by other means.

The barrister then informed the jury that he did not expect them to acquit the prisoner if they considered it their duty to do otherwise. He was not asking for clemency, but what he did demand was justice and that could only be delivered by a verdict of manslaughter.

At this stage, Mr Adolphus objected to the line of defence, claiming it had been designed so no question should be raised which would give him a right of reply.

Price had proposed to call witnesses to speak as to the character of Greenacre, but after Adolphus stated that in such circumstances he would claim a right of reply, Price declined to call any.

Price then turned his attention to the defence of Sarah Gale, a woman who, he asserted, had been placed at the mercy of the jury with no concrete evidence having been produced against her. She had not been proved to have been privy to the alleged murder or the subsequent attempt to conceal the crime. Gale had, in fact, been turned out of the house to accommodate the deceased woman and yet she was being charged with siding with, assisting and comforting the alleged murderer.

Greenacre's haste and hurry to conceal the crime was, Price claimed, to hide it from the knowledge of the woman with whom he expected to share his exile and who was to be his comfort through life, Sarah Gale. Even the witnesses that had been called had shown her character to be of sobriety and decency of conduct, notwithstanding the way in which she related to Greenacre. No one had noticed any change in the woman's behaviour that would have indicated any semblance of guilt and Price pleaded to the jury that she was entitled to their favour, indeed he demanded it on her behalf.

With an acknowledgement that he had every faith in the jury arriving at the correct verdicts, Price concluded his defence.

Judge Tindal then provided the jury with his summary of the case and some guidance as to their options regarding possible verdicts on both Greenacre and Gale. It would appear the jury had already made up their minds. Only fifteen minutes after they had retired for deliberation, the jury returned to the courtroom to deliver their verdict.

Greenacre stared at each individual juror as they passed before him, perhaps trying to glean something from their countenance, whilst Gale sat looking lost and bewildered as her fate unfolded before her.

When asked by the Clerk of Court whether they found the prisoner James Greenacre guilty or not guilty of the felony of murder with which he was charged, the jury foreman replied, 'Guilty.' The same question was asked regarding the charges brought against Sarah Gale and the same verdict was returned.

Greenacre appeared to be unmoved by the verdict, but as he was ordered to be led away, he suddenly sprung forward and began to speak. 'My Lord, I hope...' was all he managed to get out before the Judge exclaimed, 'I cannot hear you. Let them be taken back!' With that, the two prisoners were led from the dock. Before they were separated, Gale threw her arms around Greenacre and gently kissed him.

Judge Tindal thanked the jury and they, in turn, thanked him and the Sheriffs for the comfort and accommodation they had been afforded during the trial.

As news of the verdict spread among the crowds gathered outside the Court, wild cheering broke out and hats were waved in the air as if a Derby winner was being waved home.

In a departure from normal practice, to avoid the unedifying scenes that had occurred outside the courtroom the previous evening, it was decided to keep secret the time that the Recorder would announce sentencing.

The session eventually took place in the Old Bailey at 1:40pm on 12 April 1837 and at that precise time, the doors of a comparatively empty courtroom were closed to the public. Greenacre was asked by the Recorder if he wished to make a statement to the Court before sentence was pronounced upon him. Greenacre did, of course, wish to do so.

'My Lord, my unhappy condition in this unfortunate affair,' he began, 'has given rise to an abundance of evidence against me such as might be collected in any pothouse or gin shop, owing to the reports spread abroad to my prejudice, upon which the jurymen have acted.'

'It is contrary to reason,' Greenacre continued, 'that I should have meditated the death of the woman, much less that I should effect it in the manner described because of the property she had. If that had been my objective, I could have had it all on the next morning, when our marriage was to have taken place and it would be mine.'

'Where then, was my motive for murdering her. It is ....' At this point, the Recorder interrupted Greenacre and informed him that this was all material to have been raised by his lawyer at the trial but should not be pressed upon the Court now.

Greenacre was then offered the opportunity to say anything further, which he duly took.

'In the next place, I beg to say that this woman was utterly ignorant of the affair up to the time of me being taken to the police office. She had no knowledge whatever of it and is as innocent as any lady or gentleman in this Court. This I say as I am going to my grave, she is innocent. I invited her back to the house after the body was removed and she never knew anything about it. I deem it a religious duty to exculpate her from having any concern in this unfortunate affair. I have no more to say.'

In line with her stance in previous sessions, Gale declined the offer to make any statement.

The Recorder then proceeded with the passing of sentence on James Greenacre. He decided not to hold back in his condemnation of the prisoner.

'James Greenacre, after a protracted trial which endured for two entire days,' the Recorder declared in a suitably solemn tone, 'upon a patient and impartial investigation of all the circumstances connected with your case, a jury of your country have found themselves inevitably compelled to find you guilty of the dreadful offence for which you were indicted.'

The tone of the Recorder's address darkened even further as he recounted a tale of; odious notoriety in the annals of cruelty and crime; concealment of mangled and dismembered portions of the victim; blows to the skull and eye of the victim; the severing of the head as blood still flowed through the woman's body and the further mutilation of the, still warm, corpse.

Although Greenacre had attempted to conceal the crime from the eyes of man, the Recorder offered, the all-seeing eye of God was cognisant of the deed and man became the agent of its discovery. Warming to the religious theme, he then went on to quote to Greenacre, a man he considered to be 'not devoid of education, of reasoning facilities and strength of mind', a passage from 'The Anthology of Religion, Natural and Revealed.'

What an impassive looking Greenacre was making of this we cannot know, but he was implored by the Recorder to turn with a humble and penitent heart to the source of all hope and mercy, the blessed Redeemer of mankind.

There was to be no hope and mercy in the courtroom that day, however, as the Recorder proclaimed, 'It now only remains for me to pass upon you the dreadful sentence of the law. That sentence is that you be taken from hence to the prison from which you came and from thence to a place of execution, where you shall be hanged by the neck until dead.'

Mercifully, the Recorder informed Sarah Gale he did not intend to aggravate the sufferings she was about to endure with any observations of his own. He noted Greenacre's declaration of her innocence but offered that she had united herself to the man, sharing his society and bed, comforting, assisting and sheltering him, without being joined to him by any moral or religious tie. He then pointed out she had been found in possession of the murdered woman's earrings, together with several other items identified as having previously belonged to the deceased.

Informing Gale of his belief the jury had come to a justly grounded verdict in her case, the Recorder proceeded to pass sentence and declared that Sarah Gale should, 'be transported beyond the sea to such a place as His Majesty with the advice of his Privy Council shall direct and appoint, for the rest of your natural life.'

The prisoners were then led in silence from the bar and taken to their respective cells.

On 26 April 1837, the Recorder made a report to the King concerning seven prisoners under sentence of death at Newgate Prison. The King declared he was graciously pleased to extend his Royal mercy to all but one, James Greenacre, whose execution had been set for 2 May.

The Ordinary delivered the King's decision to Greenacre, who took the news calmly and replied, 'It cannot be helped. I am sacrificed through prejudice and falsehood.' The Ordinary then expressed his hope Greenacre would spend the period between the moment the communication was made and the time of his execution in earnest and hearty prayer.

'Nothing but inward prayer will suit my condition,' Greenacre replied. 'I have confidence in the mercy of God and will trust to that. I care not a pin for death, but I abhor the thought of going out of the world branded a wilful murdered. I committed no murder.'

'The blood of the unfortunate woman is on your hands, for it was by your means she came to her death,' the Ordinary said.

'Yes, but it might as well be said I murdered her if a cartwheel passed over her and I, afterwards, committed the mutilation. I have fallen as a sacrifice to the press.'

With that, the Ordinary handed Greenacre a book of prayer. Greenacre thanked the man for his humanity and attention, then was finally left in peace in the solitude of his cell.

Although Greenacre's fate was sealed, there was no abatement in the public's thirst for knowledge of the man and the press were only too happy to provide them with the stories they craved.

One such story involved events that had taken place barely one month after the death and mutilation of Hannah Brown. On 23 January 1837, Greenacre had placed an advertisement in The Times newspaper which read as follows:-

'Wanted, a partner who can commit three hundred pounds

to join the advertiser in a patent to bring forward a newly-invented machine of great public benefit that is certain of realising an ample reward.

Applications, by letter only, post-paid, for J.G. at 1 Tudor Place, Tottenham Court Road.'

Among the responses was that from a woman of some wealth, whose name was withheld by the newspaper, which caught Greenacre's attention. The two, subsequently, met on several occasions, though no concrete arrangements were agreed.

This prompted Greenacre to step up his game and he changed tact with the following letter to the woman, dated 4 February 1837:-

'Dear Madam, having had several letters in response to my advertisement, yours is the third to which I have replied for an interview and is the last one I shall answer. I advertised in The Times newspaper for a partner with three hundred pounds to join me in a patent to take forward a newly-invented machine, of which I have enclosed you printed specification from scientific gentlemen of property, each anxious to co-operate with me in it.

Upon mature consideration and by the advice of my friends, I have decided not to throw away the half of this most important discovery for the trifling sum of three hundred pounds, as it is certainly worth many thousands. It is, therefore, my wish to meet with a female companion, with a small capital, one with whom a mutual and tender attachment might be formed, who would share with me in those advantageous pecuniary prospects which are now before me and thereby secure the advantages of my own production.

No one can have a greater aversion than myself to

advertising for a wife, nevertheless, this advertisement was intended to give an opportunity by which I might make proposals of an honourable nature to one whom I might prefer as a companion for life. It may be, however, that the first impression from our short interviews has left very different feelings towards me than those by which I am influenced to write this letter to you. I hope otherwise, or at least that you will not yield to any unfavourable conjectures relative to the moderation of my views regarding the sum of money I named in my advertisement.

It is, I think, sufficient to convince you, or any of your advisors and friends, that property forms but a small share of my hopes and objectives in turning towards a partner for life. I am a widower of thirty-eight years of age, without any encumbrance and in the possession of some small income arising from the rent of some houses. I was sixteen years in a large way of business which I relinquished about three years ago, but have lost much of my property by assisting others and confiding too strongly in the professions of pretended friends.

Under these circumstances, I am induced to seek a partner, or a companion with a small sum, to co-operate with me in securing the advantages of this machine which will be a great public benefit and which has long been attempted by many scientific persons and is certain of realising a competency. Having given you this plain statement of my situation, I beg leave to add that my mind is thoroughly fixed upon making you the future object of my affections and constant regard.

If you should feel disposed to favour my sincere and honourable intentions, I shall take the liberty of calling upon you and hope you will divest your mind of any idea beyond that of the most sacred candour and honourable intentions on my part. Should you feel disposed to communicate any remarks on the subject by letter, I hope that you will do so.

Excuse the dissimulation by which I have obtained an introduction to you and believe that my present proposal is dictated by every honourable and affectionate feeling towards you. I am, dear Madam, yours most sincerely, James Greenacre.'

At the time of composing the letter, the sincere and honourable James Greenacre was still cohabiting with Sarah Gale, still actually married to his fourth wife in America (a fact that had since been verified by Inspector Feltham) and still, at least metaphorically, stained in the blood of Hannah Brown. The arrest of Greenacre in March 1837 at least prevented any possibility of a new tragedy developing with the mystery woman who had become the latest focus of his attentions.

On 2 May 1837, vast crowds gathered outside the debtor's door of Newgate Prison to witness the execution of James Greenacre. The crowds had begun to assemble the previous evening and a carnival atmosphere had been maintained throughout the night, aided by the setting up of an actual funfair.

As dawn approached, a group of pickpockets descended upon the crowded public houses and coffee shops and the police were fully stretched in trying to dispel them while coping with the ever-increasing numbers of members of the public filling the streets. Local bakers, selling 'penny sandwiches' and 'Greenacre tarts', mingled with artists selling drawings of the condemned man and with hawkers selling the entirely fictional 'true life story and confessions of James Greenacre'.

At 4am, workmen emerged from the yawning jaws of the debtor's door and began to erect the scaffold from which the death sentence would be carried out. Shortly afterwards, to three hearty cheers from the crowd, the platform was wheeled out. Similar cheering greeted each stage of the assembly of the apparatus, with a special cheer reserved for the hangman as he carried out his testing.

As the morning continued, the increase in numbers was unrelenting and many women and children were passed over the heads of the crowd to escape being crushed, as the barriers police had put into place failed to cope.

The tolling of the bell at nearby St Sepulchre's Church, signalling 7:45am, sent the crowd into a frenzy which was maintained until the appointed time of 8am when the hangman and his assistant remounted the platform and carried out their final checks. A cry of 'hats off' was heard and it was a bare-headed crowd that greeted the condemned man with a volley of hatred as he made his way up the steps to the platform.

Greenacre quickly placed himself into the hands of the executioner, who wasted no time in completing the preparations for his death. The Ordinary read the commencing verse of the service, but before it was completed the bolt was withdrawn and James Greenacre fell to his fate. It had taken less than two minutes from his first appearance on the platform until his passing.

It was estimated that over 20,000 people witnessed the execution of James Greenacre. The speed at which the execution had been carried out was the result of a request from the condemned man that had been granted by the sheriffs.

Sarah Gale was removed from Newgate Prison to Woolwich on 26 June 1837, where she remained for a short time until her transportation, together with her child, to New South Wales. She would remain in Australia until her death in 1888.

The English Ballad, 'Sarah Gale's Lament', was written on the subject in 1837:-

'As I walked down by the walls of Newgate,
I thought I heard a female say,
I am doomed my days to linger,
In the land of Botany Bay.
Will no one on me have compassion,
While I tell my mournful tale?
In grief lamenting and repenting,
In despair is Sarah Gale.

I did cohabit with Greenacre,
When I knew he had a wife,
Long with him, I have resided,
A most abandoned wretched life.
But now from him I'm separated,
Left to tell a dismal tale,
Will no one on me show compassion?
Sad's the fate of Sarah Gale.

I was brought up by honest parents,
Instructed was in virtuous ways,
But while I live, I shall be lost,
Curse the sad and fatal day,

I with Greenacre got acquainted,
Oh, listen to my mournful tale,
Confined within the walls of Newgate,
Weeping is poor Sarah Gale.

I with Greenacre was arrested,
Scoffed by everyone around,
Tried before a British Jury,
For the death of Hannah Brown.
For concealing, I was convicted,
Oh, what a sad and dismal tale,
Doomed a wretched life to linger,
Is the fate of Sarah Gale.

Alas, that fatal Tuesday morning,
At the hour of eight o'clock,
The dreadful groans the shouts and hisses,
Did my very bosom shock.
When Greenacre on the scaffold died,
Oh, what a sad and dismal tale,
Can anyone describe the feelings,
Of the wretched Sarah Gale?

But now his life has paid the forfeit,
He died a death of public scorn,
And I am left a wretched creature,
In agony, I weep forlorn.
In a foreign land, I am doomed to linger
Out my days, oh, what a tale,
Sad was the day that James Greenacre

Got acquainted with Sarah Gale.

You females all by the like take warning,
Rich and poor, high and low,
What troubles you may yet encounter,
It's very hard for you to know.
Strive to walk in the paths of virtue,
Take a lesson from this mournful tale,
Sad was the day I saw Greenacre,
For he has ruined Sarah Gale.'

The notoriety of the couple would earn them one of the very first displays in Madame Tussauds Chamber of Horrors in London.

Although the Metropolitan Police had been formed in 1829, it would be a further thirteen years before a Detective Branch would be established.

During the period in which the Hannah Brown investigation took place, 1836-37, the Metropolitan Force was divided by area. There were, initially, seventeen Divisions, A - Westminster; B - Chelsea; C - Mayfair and Soho; D - Marylebone; E - Holborn; F - Kensington; G - Kings Cross; H - Stepney; K - West Ham; L - Lambeth; M - Southwark; N - Islington; P - Peckham; R - Greenwich; S - Hampstead; T - Hammersmith and V - Wandsworth.

Although the formation of a separate Detective Branch was still several years down the road, the shape it would take was being set by officers such as Inspector George Feltham and his able Sergeant, Samuel Pegler. The lessons learned from the thorough and painstaking investigations carried out by men such as these would go a long way towards establishing the blueprint for the future investigations of Scotland Yard.

2 ROAD KILL

The home of the Kent family, Road Hill House, was something of a house of mystery even before the events that were about to unfold in June 1860.

The village of Road (to be found on present-day maps as Rode) is located between the counties of Wiltshire and Somerset, having transferred from the former to the latter over the course of time. Even the village itself seems to be hard to pin down.

Samuel Saville Kent, an inspector of factories, resided at the elegant Georgian mansion with his wife, Mary. The other Kent family members living in the household in 1860 were; eldest daughter Mary Ann Alice, aged 29; Elizabeth, aged 27; Constance Emily, aged 16; William Saville, aged 15; Mary Amelia Saville, aged 5; Francis Saville, aged 3 and Eveline, aged 1. The eldest four children were from Kent's previous marriage to his late wife Mary Ann.

The members of the household staff who resided on the premises were Elizabeth Gough, the nursemaid, Sarah Cox, the housemaid, and Sarah Kerslake, the cook.

Mr and Mrs Kent shared their room on the first floor with Mary Amelia. Elizabeth Gough shared a room with Francis and Eveline. The housemaid and cook slept in a room next door to Constance's room and William slept in a room located towards the back of the property on the second floor.

Kent's wife had previously worked for the family as a live-in governess and had served for a period of thirteen years during the lifetime of the first Mrs Kent. Mary had been given full charge of the children during the latter part of that period of service, as Mrs Kent was thought to be suffering from some serious mental health problems. Samuel Kent would go on to marry his former governess some sixteen months after the tragic death of Mary Ann, though according to local gossip they had 'been together' for a long time before then.

On the morning of 30 June 1860, life for the Kent family was about to take a dramatic turn and their lives were destined to never be the same again. As the others in the household slept soundly, young Francis was plucked from the warmth and safety of his cosy little cot.

The first person to notice the child was missing was his nursemaid, Elizabeth Gough. Gough stirred from sleep at around 5am and as she cast a bleary eye around the room, she spied the empty cot. When she had recovered from her initial shock, the nursemaid calmed herself and concluded that the child must have been taken from the room by his mother. The removal of the child to sleep beside his parents was, apparently, a regular occurrence in the household.

Several hours would pass before the metaphorical alarm bells started ringing, as it came to light the child was not with his mother and could not be found anywhere else within the house. A full-scale search of the grounds surrounding the house was hastily organised and began at about 8am.

Just as the search started to get underway, Mr Kent, somewhat curiously in the eyes of the members of the search party, had his carriage brought to the front of the house then set off at pace towards Trowbridge. There he would report the loss of the child to local Police-Superintendent John Foley. For reasons best known to himself, Kent was absolutely convinced his son had been kidnapped.

Within a relatively short period of time, two of the members of the public that had willingly joined the search for the missing child, William Nutt, a local shoemaker, and Thomas Benger, a local farmer, made a horrific discovery.

As the two men peered through the part-opened door of an outhouse that had served as a privy for the staff, they caught sight of a blood-soaked blanket. Consumed by an overwhelming feeling of trepidation, the men opened the door and edged towards the toilet. Inside, trapped between the crude toilet seat and the dark hole below, lay the tiny body of young Francis Saville Kent.

The child, who was still dressed in his little nightshirt, had knife wounds on his chest and hands. As the two men tried to carefully remove the body from the dank pit, their eyes fixed upon a clean cut that ran across the boy's throat. The cut was so deep that when the horrified men tried to lift him, the child's head almost separated from his body.

On Monday 9 July, the Magistrates of the Trowbridge division set up private meetings at the Temperance Hall in Road to carry out an investigation into the murder of the child, Francis Saville Kent. The Chief Constables of Wiltshire and Somerset, together with the Police Superintendents of Frome and Trowbridge were also present.

Interviews were held with Mr Kent, the three live-in maids, the man servant, a boy who cleaned the knives, the washerwoman, William Nutt and Thomas Benger. The Magistrates seemed a bit more reluctant to obtain statements from the family members of the household, indeed no statements whatsoever were taken from Mrs Mary Kent and from Constance Kent, one of the daughters from Mr Kent's previous marriage.

Mrs Kent, who was heavily pregnant at the time, was perhaps understandably considered to be in no fit state to be interviewed, due to concerns about her own well-being and that of the child she was carrying. The consideration that sixteen-year-old Constance was too delicate a flower to face a judicial examination was rather more difficult to justify.

The Magistrates were extremely reluctant to release to the public any details of the evidence they had gathered at this stage. Despite a direct appeal to the Bench from the local press, the Magistrates held firm to their resolution to carry out their Inquiry in private. However, due to the nature of the crime, it was not going to be possible to keep a cap on the proceedings for long and the national newspapers picked up on the story.

The Morning Post was particularly scathing and raised many points they felt were not being adequately addressed at the Inquiry. The newspaper expressed the view that all the evidence clearly pointed to the culprit being someone from within the household. They also made clear their belief that the local Magistrates were not qualified to carry out the investigations into the murder and called on the Secretary of State to intervene.

One of the many pitfalls of attempting to shroud major murder Inquiries in a cloak of secrecy is that the vacuum left by a lack of available facts is soon filled by the circulation of rumours. Within a short time, so many rumours were afloat that the local police were instructed, at the request of Mr Kent, to caution people as to the potential consequences of what they were saying.

This hush-hush Inquiry was being held during a period when the British class system was firmly in place and the outcome would have likely come as no great surprise. On

Tuesday 10 July, the boy's nursemaid, Elizabeth Gough, was taken into custody on suspicion of having been involved in his murder. Gough was remanded until Friday 20 July.

Among those outside of the Inquiry, there was a general view the nursemaid was innocent. Indeed, one member of the local police force engaged in the case stated, off the record, that he did not believe there was a shred of evidence to warrant her arrest.

In the meantime, the ever-increasing media interest had pressed the Home Secretary into action and he decided it was time to call on the expertise of Scotland Yard. Detective-Inspector Jonathan Whicher, an original member of the Detective Branch established in 1842, was called in to assist in the investigation.

Whicher arrived in Trowbridge on Sunday 15 July and proceeded to Road on Monday to meet with the Magistrates conducting the case. After hearing of the evidence gathered against the nursemaid, or more accurately the lack of any evidence, Whicher convinced the Magistrates to bring Elizabeth Gough before the Bench and to release her from custody. Elizabeth was informed she was at liberty to go anywhere she pleased, but she indicated her intention to return to her duties in the Kent household.

A reward of two hundred pounds was put up for information that would lead to the conviction of the perpetrator, one hundred pounds to be provided by the Government and the other one hundred pounds by Mr Kent. A pardon was also offered to any accomplice who came forward with information about the person who had committed the murder.

After Gough's release, the investigation pretty much

started again from scratch and Whicher decided the house and grounds should be re-examined and searched. Everyone who lived or worked in the house was interviewed and called on to state exactly what they knew.

A new and now very public Inquiry was held on Friday 20 July.

Inspector Whicher took everyone by surprise when he arrived with the murdered child's half-sister, Constance Kent, in tow. A tearful Constance had been brought directly from Road Hill House to the Temperance Hall. The trembling girl was placed in a seat in front of the Magistrate's table, sandwiched between Whicher and Superintendent Woolfe.

As word of Constance Kent's apprehension spread, the hall very quickly filled with curious locals and news-hungry members of the press. Whicher's formal charge was read to the Magistrates by the clerk:-

'I have been engaged since Sunday last in investigating the circumstances connected with the murder of Francis Saville Kent, which took place on the night of Friday 29 June last, at the house of his father, situated at Road, in the county of Wilts.

From my examination of the premises, the scene of the murder, and from inquiries and information received, I have reason to believe the said murder was perpetrated by an inmate of the house and I suspect Miss Constance Kent is implicated in the crime. I, therefore, request a warrant to apprehend her.'

Elizabeth Gough, no doubt greatly relieved to no longer be the chief suspect, was then sworn in. Gough provided the Inquiry with a full account of her movements on the night of the child's disappearance. 'I am a nursemaid in the service of

Mr Kent. I recollect 29 June last. I had charge of the deceased child and put him to bed, as usual, at about 8pm. I saw him sleeping in his cot, with his face to the wall, at a little after 11pm. I then retired to rest, as usual. Mrs Kent came up, about half an hour after, and shut the door when she left. I missed the child the following morning, at about 5am. I did not wake till that time after I went to sleep.'

'The little girl was lying uncovered and I got up and looked across and saw the little boy was gone. I lay down again and at 6am I went to Mrs Kent's room and knocked there, but got no answer. I, afterwards, went to Mrs Kent's room a second time, at about 7:15am. In the interval, I had got water for the second child and had dressed her. Mrs Kent was then in the dressing-room. I communicated the loss to her and afterwards saw the child brought into the house. He was, then, quite dead.'

William Nutt was the next witness to testify and he stated, 'I am a shoemaker, residing at Road Hill. On the morning of 30 June, a man called and told me Mr Kent had lost his child. I went out and saw Mr Kent going to Trowbridge. I then went to the house with a man named Benger. We came to the bottom of the plantation and I said we would look for a dead child if the living one was not found. We went to the closet and to our horror found a pool of blood on the floor. I said, 'Oh, Benger, it is as I predicted.' I then went to the house and asked for a candle and when I had got it and returned to Benger, he said 'Here is the dear little thing.'

'Benger took out the child and a blanket and took them into the house. The child's throat was cut. To our horror and amazement, when it was lifted its little head almost fell off. The body was taken into the kitchen. Miss Constance Kent and Miss Elizabeth Kent came into the room. I can't describe their horror. I and the constable went round the premises but could discern nothing more. The servants and neighbours also came in and saw the child. That is all I know.'

Inspector Whicher then rose again and said, 'In company with Captain Meredith, Superintendent Foley and other members of the police force, I have made an examination of the premises and believe the murderer was some inmate of the house. From many inquiries that I have made and from information received, I sent for Constance Kent, on Monday last, to her bedroom.'

The Inspector continued. 'Having previously examined Miss Kent's drawers and found a list of her linen, which I now produce, in which were enumerated, among other things, three nightdresses as belonging to her, I said to her, 'Is this a list of your linen?' She replied, 'Yes'. I said, 'In whose writing is it?' She said, 'It is my own writing.' I said, 'Here are listed three nightdresses, where are they?' She replied, 'I have two, the other was lost in the wash the week after the murder.' She then brought me the two which I now produce. I also saw a nightdress and cap on her bed and asked whose they were. She said, 'They are my sister's.' The two she brought me had been worn.'

Whicher went on, 'This afternoon, I again proceeded to the house and sent for the prisoner into the dining-room. I said, 'I am a police officer and I hold a warrant for your apprehension, charging you with the murder of your brother Francis Saville Kent which I shall read to you.' I then read the warrant to her and she commenced crying and said, 'I am innocent,' which she repeated several times.'

'I accompanied her to her bedroom,' Whither continued, 'where she put on her bonnet and mantle and I then brought her to this place. She made no further remarks to me. I now ask for a remand for a few days and on the next occasion, I believe I shall be able to show the *animus* which existed between the prisoner and the deceased. It will also allow me time to search for the missing nightdress, which if in existence may possibly be found. An adjournment to Wednesday or Thursday next, I think, will be ample time.'

The prisoner was remanded until the following Friday and was then transported to Devizes Jail in the custody of Whicher and Woolfe.

Mr Kent promptly set about bringing in a top legal team to defend his daughter against the charge of murder. Kent employed the services of William Dunn, a solicitor based in Frome. More significantly, he also brought onboard Mr Peter Edlin of the Western Court Circuit.

The police resumed their extensive searches in and around the property at Road Hill House trying to trace the missing nightdress. Inspector Whicher felt his case would be weakened greatly if he was unable to present the nightdress as evidence at the Inquiry.

The Inquiry resumed on Friday 27 June with the vital evidence, sadly, still absent. A pale looking Constance Kent, accompanied by the Governor of Devizes Jail, arrived at the Temperance Hall at around 11am. After hugging her father, Constance took her allotted place and sat, quietly sobbing, as the hall was opened to the public and quickly filled to capacity.

The witnesses were re-sworn and Elizabeth Gough was again first to be questioned. She had little to add to her previous testimony but clarified that the reason she had taken so long to report the child missing was because she was sure he was with Mrs Kent. Elizabeth added that prior to going to

Mrs Kent's room on the first occasion, she had read a chapter from the Bible and had said her prayers.

In conclusion, Elizabeth stated that during the time she had been in Mr Kent's service, she had never heard Constance say anything unkind towards the dead child.

A fresh witness, Emma Moody, a school classmate of Constance at Beckington, was then called. When asked if she had ever heard Constance express any feelings towards the child, Emma replied, 'She expressed jealousy. She has said she disliked it and that she liked to tease the younger children.'

Emma continued. 'I said on one occasion, 'Won't it be nice to go home shortly?' She said, 'Yes, perhaps to your home, but mine is different.' She said the second family were much better treated than herself and her brother, William.'

Edlin objected to this line of questioning and complained that the clerk for the Magistrates, the aptly named Mr Clarke, who was putting the questions to the witness, was exceeding his duty by pressing these inquiries. This objection was met by a round of applause from the locals in the gallery. The chairman was unmoved by the spontaneous outburst however and overruled the objection on the grounds it was too vague.

Inspector Whicher then advised the Inquiry that he had visited Emma Moody at her home. During his interview with the girl, Whicher had asked her if she was able to identify a piece of flannel he had brought with him. Emma had been unable identify the item and Whicher had then presented the girl with a summons to attend the Inquiry.

Joshua Parsons, the surgeon who was called on to inspect the body of the murdered child and to carry out the post-mortem, was next to make a statement. He provided a graphic description of the state of the body, which had suffered wounds to the chest and hands as well as an incision to the throat extending from one ear to the other. Parsons expressed the view that it would have taken considerable strength to have made the specific wound to the chest. He also said he had examined the linen in Constance's room and believed he had seen a clean nightdress in the drawers.

Another of Constance's school classmates, Louise Hatheritt, was next. Louise revealed that Constance had said to her there was a partiality shown towards the younger children by the parents. Constance had also spoken to Hatheritt of her brother William's dislike of having to push around the perambulators of the younger children. Constance had also claimed to have overheard her father stating his youngest son would become a finer man than William would ever be.

Sarah Cox, the housemaid, then provided her statement. She spoke of her routine of gathering the laundry and confirmed she had seen nothing unusual regarding the much-discussed nightdress. Cox said that shortly after the murder of the child, Constance had appeared at the door of the lumber-room whilst the laundry was being prepared for onward transmission to the washer-woman, Mrs Holly.

Constance had told Cox she thought she may have left her purse in her slip pocket, but, despite a thorough search of the laundry basket, it was nowhere to be seen. Constance had then asked Cox if she would fetch her a glass of water. While Cox set off to get the water, Constance had been left on her own in the room for a minute or two. Cox next told the Inquiry she was certain that she had put Constance's nightdress into the laundry basket, but could not swear it had ever left the house as she was not present at the time the laundry was picked up.

In reply to a question from Edlin, Sarah Cox answered that she had never, at any time, heard Constance speak ill of her little brother.

Next up was Esther Holly, the laundress. Holly had collected the laundry on the Monday after the murder. She had later been made aware of the fact a nightdress had gone missing. Holly claimed to have opened the laundry basket within five minutes of arriving home and confirmed it had only contained two of Constance's nightdresses at that time.

Edlin then raised another objection, claiming the Magistrates were conducting the Inquiry as if it were a prosecution and were allowing questions that would have been ruled inadmissible in a Court of Law. The exasperated chairman replied that the Magistrates had no intention of acting as prosecutors but were merely trying to conduct an investigation, one which was being continually interrupted by Mr Edlin. Edlin was not for letting go and submitted to the Bench that, 'In a case where a young lady was on remand, charged with a wilful murder, no question ought to be put to witnesses which would be inadmissible in the prosecution of so serious a charge.'

When Edlin finally returned to his seat, Esther Holly continued with her statement. Holly claimed to have sent word back to the house as soon as she had discovered Constance's third nightdress was not in the laundry basket. She had been taken by surprise, therefore, when she received word that Mr Kent was threatening to have a warrant issued against her if she did not return the missing item within forty-eight hours.

Holly concluded her statement by revealing the police had later carried out a thorough search of her house but had found nothing incriminating.

With that, the Magistrates announced that they had no further witnesses to introduce.

Edlin wasted no time in requesting the immediate release of Constance Kent. In a typically barnstorming speech, the bulldog-like lawyer outlined his reasons.

Not one shred of evidence had been produced and not one word said that would point the finger of blame towards his client, Edlin claimed. It was his belief an atrocious murder had been followed by a judicial murder no less atrocious. Applying further pressure, the fiery lawyer threatened that if the real culprit was not apprehended, it would never be forgotten that the young lady had been dragged off, like a common felon, to Devizes Prison.

Without bothering to disguise his contempt, Edlin claimed the young lady's prospects in life had been blighted, solely on the suspicions of a police inspector acting under the influence of the reward on offer. The lawyer expressed his conviction that the facts regarding the missing nightdress had been cleared up to the satisfaction of any right-thinking person.

Returning to his tactic of attacking the actions of Inspector Whicher, Edlin said he believed the hunting down of his client's school-fellows had reflected ineffable disgrace upon those who had been the means of bringing them before the Inquiry, claiming the evidence of the girls had not shown anything like *animus* on the part of his client towards the deceased child.

Edlin finished by suggesting it would reflect badly on the Bench if they were to pursue the case against his client, as weak a case as he had ever heard.

Spontaneous applause again broke out from the gallery, though this was quickly suppressed by the chairman. After a brief consultation, the Magistrates announced that Miss Constance Kent was to be discharged upon her father entering into recognisances of two hundred pounds for her further appearance if called upon.

Somebody had to take the fall for the collapse of the case and Inspector Whicher was effectively sidelined. The predictable backlash arrived quickly.

In a parliamentary debate on the salaries and expenses for the Metropolitan Police, Sir George Bowyer rose to say he had received information regarding a great many abuses that prevailed within the Metropolitan Police Force. One of the chief complaints made to him was that persons who were unfit for such positions were being promoted to be Inspectors without undergoing any examinations.

Just in case there was any doubt as to whom he may have been referring, Bowyer continued by offering that the recent investigations regarding the Road murder afforded striking proof of the unsuitability of some of the present officers. Finally getting around to naming Inspector Whicher, Bowyer went on to say that in his view, the officer had arrested a young lady on the slightest possible grounds, merely because one of her nightdresses happened to be missing.

The upper-classes were circling their waggons.

Sir George Lewis, the Home Secretary who had assigned the case to Scotland Yard, replied to Bowyer and said he did not think it appropriate to refer to this ongoing case, as it was difficult for him to remain silent when such remarks were being made. He had, of course, he stated, been appraised of all the facts relating to the case, but did not think he would be justified in disclosing them to the Committee.

Public interest in the murder was on the rise and the two policemen stationed at Road Hill House were kept on their toes trying to stop people from encroaching onto the private grounds. Unwelcome visitors were appearing from nearby towns just to catch a glimpse of the picturesque little village that had hit the national newspaper headlines.

News broke that Mrs Kent had given birth to a child. Although the baby was born prematurely, both mother and child were said to be doing well.

The police began another round of searches, but again nothing was found to implicate anyone in the murder. They then carried out an experiment to replicate the scene where Constance had sent the housemaid for a glass of water. There had been accusations that Constance had removed the nightdress from the laundry basket during the time she was alone in the room. The fetching of the water was timed at under two minutes. Constance explained to the policemen that she had not gone for the water herself as she had been concerned about the number of strangers wandering about the house at the time. She claimed to have been very nervous after having just provided testimony before the Coroner.

Elizabeth Gough gave notice of her intention to leave Mr Kent's service and notice from the housemaid, Sara Cox, quickly followed.

The testimony Gough had provided at the Inquiries was re-examined by the police. When she had been brought before the Magistrates, the nursemaid had said she had not noticed the blanket was missing from the child's cot until she had seen it wrapped around the body when it had been brought into the kitchen. Thomas Benger, the parish constable and the county policeman all claimed to have clearly heard her say during the initial search that the child had been carried off in a blanket.

The case then took a dramatic new twist when a man in London confessed to the murder.

The man who had confessed to the killing of Francis Saville Kent said his Christian names were Edmund John and that he was a railway navvy from Pimlico, London. He declined to provide his surname.

Edmund claimed to have been in Road searching for work when he'd been approached by a man and woman who offered him a considerable sum of money to dispose of a child. Edmund said he had needed the money so he had accepted the offer and had murdered the child. He had, he continued, originally planned to bury the body under a garden hedge, but had changed his mind and then decided to leave it in the location where it was subsequently discovered. Edmund stated that he knew the names of the man and woman but would not reveal them until he got to Bath. He was brought before the Magistrate in Stony Stratford, then taken into custody in Trowbridge.

There was a nagging suspicion that the man, who had seemed quite plausible in conversation, had confessed to the murder in the hope of obtaining free transportation to Bath. Inspector Whicher was given the task of uncovering the truth and his investigations revealed the man to be Edmund John Gagg.

When Gagg was brought before the Magistrates in Trowbridge, he declared that everything he had said in his confession was, in fact, untrue. When asked the perfectly reasonable question as to why he had made the statement in the first place, Gagg claimed to have been deeply troubled and feeling suicidal at the time. Throwing himself on the mercy of the Magistrates, Gagg whimpered that his life continued to be a burden to him.

Inspector Whicher revealed he had made enquiries in London and had spoken to Gagg's wife. The woman had declared she was only too happy to be living without her worthlessness husband and raising their children on her own. She had also made it clear to the Inspector she had no intention of taking him back after this latest escapade.

The Magistrates decided, in an act of extreme generosity, that although they were tempted to punish Gagg, they would instead pay his fare back to his home parish in Westminster.

As the case appeared to be stalling yet again, an application was lodged by Samuel Kent's counsel for a fresh Inquest to be held. This was deemed not to be legally possible. A formal application was then lodged to have a special commission set up to look at the case anew, but this was also turned down on the grounds that it was 'unusual and impractical'.

Then, out of the blue, another confession arrived. This one came from a labourer in the south of Ireland who professed to have aided Constance in committing the murder. The man said he could produce the missing nightdress on receipt of money for his fare to England. Once bitten, twice shy, the Magistrates decided they had paid enough free transportation costs to complete chancers for the present.

If, at first, you don't succeed, try her again.

Following a private investigation, carried out at the request of the Wiltshire Magistrates under the sanction of the Home Secretary, Elizabeth Gough was re-arrested. The investigation had been led by Mr Slack, a solicitor from Bath. Having completed his enquiries, Slack had forwarded the depositions of the various witnesses to the Attorney-General. On the advice of his own counsel, Mr Kent had refused permission for any members of his family to be interviewed at the offices of Mr Slack. Under tight restrictions, these interviews had eventually been carried out at Road Hill House.

Elizabeth Gough was taken to Devizes Jail to await yet another Inquiry, one at which Mr Slack would instruct the prosecution, Mr Edlin would watch the proceedings for Mr Kent and Gough would be represented by an eminent lawyer, Mr Ribton.

On 1 October 1860, Elizabeth Gough was brought before Magistrates in Trowbridge by Superintendent Woolfe, to again face the charge of the murder of Francis Saville Kent. Mr Saunders, appearing on behalf of Mr Slack and the Crown, made an opening statement in which he claimed to be in possession of sufficient evidence to convince the Inquiry of Elizabeth's guilt.

As if Inspector Whicher hadn't suffered enough abuse, the prosecutor felt it necessary to highlight the previous apprehension of Constance Kent in connection with the murder. Saunders said that having carefully examined all aspects of the case, he believed Constance to be as clear of suspicion as any of the gentlemen he now had the honour of addressing.

Saunders went over all the events that had taken place on the night of the murder and said he had been led to the firm conclusion that due to the weight of the child, one person could not have carried out the murder on their own. Given that she had shared a room with the victim, he believed the nursemaid must have, in some way, been complicit in the matter.

Before any witnesses could be called, Mr Ribton pointed out that he had heard no new facts in Saunders' statement and, in truth, Elizabeth was being charged on the same evidence upon which she had previously been apprehended and discharged. On the grounds of *nemo debet bis vexari* (no-one should be twice tried upon the same set of facts), Ribton offered that the Inquiry should not continue.

The Magistrates made clear their belief that new facts were to be introduced in the evidence to be presented before the Bench and said it was their duty to hear them.

The first witness to be called was Samuel Kent, who admitted under questioning from Ribton that his statement was basically unchanged from those he had made previously. Kent did attempt to explain some of the actions he himself had taken after he had heard the news that the child was missing. He claimed to have gone directly to Trowbridge, rather than searching for the missing child, because he was convinced the child had been removed from the premises. This conviction was based on threats made by former servants that had fallen foul of Mr Kent and had been dismissed under acrimonious circumstances. The police had later tracked down the servants and had found them to have cast-iron alibis.

Next up was Mrs Kent, who spoke of how surprised she had been when Elizabeth had asked her if she'd taken the child into her own room. Mrs Kent claimed Elizabeth was fully aware the child was too heavy for her to carry and stated bluntly that she would never have removed him while the nursemaid was asleep.

Sarah Cox was then called and provided a short statement that added little to the proceedings. On hearing Cox had been interviewed for over three hours by Mr Slack during his investigations, Ribton witheringly remarked, 'You must have told him a great deal more than you have told us.'

The Inquiry was then adjourned until the following day.

As day two of the Inquiry began, it came as no surprise the gallery was again packed.

Statements were taken from Sarah Kerslake, the cook, James Halcolme, gardener and groom, Emily Doel, former assistant nurse, Constance Kent, James Morgan, parish constable of Road, Alfred Urch, of the Somerset County Constabulary, Henry Heritage, of the Wiltshire Constabulary, William Nutt, shoemaker and parish clerk, Thomas Benger, farmer, John Foley, Superintendent of Wiltshire Constabulary and Francis Woolfe, another Wiltshire Superintendent.

It was a busy day in which a lot of old ground was covered, though some new information did come to light. The two police constables, Morgan and Urch, revealed they had been locked in the kitchen for several hours on the evening the body had been discovered. Apparently, Mr Kent had told them he did not want them wandering around the house unaccompanied.

Another issue raised was the fact the family dog had remained silent throughout the night of the murder. The dog was known for barking loudly at any strangers that caught his eye, though he did not tend to bark at those familiar to him.

Ribton was unimpressed and claimed too little in the way of additional evidence had been produced that would in any way implicate the prisoner. The chairman replied that the Inquiry had a duty to go patiently through every piece of evidence that was presented.

The day's proceedings were then brought to a close.

Day three began with a statement from William Saville Kent, who helpfully informed the Magistrates that he had pretty much seen and heard nothing.

Mr Parsons, the local surgeon, then followed and was asked by Ribton if he had added anything new in the statement he had provided to Mr Slack. Parsons replied that he did not know. The standard of the evidence appeared to be on a downward spiral.

After Ribton had finished questioning him, Parsons expressed a wish to make a statement which he claimed might affect the prisoner as well as Mr Kent. After discussions between the Magistrates and the lawyers, it was agreed that Parsons should put the statement in writing and communicate it privately to the Magistrates. Parsons wrote his statement on a slip of paper and handed it to the Magistrates, who quickly expressed the view that it contained nothing requiring further inquiry. On seeing the note, the two lawyers agreed and Parsons was promptly dismissed.

The Inquiry continued and statements were taken from Captain Meredith, Chief Constable of Wiltshire County Constabulary and Eliza Dallimore, who had been called on to assist in questioning the female inhabitants of the house. There then followed a debate about whether questions should be put to five-year-old Mary Amelia Kent, who had shared a room with the murdered child and the nursemaid. In the end, it was decided there would be no value in doing so.

The proceedings were adjourned until the following day when Ribton would address the Magistrates on behalf of the prisoner.

Day four arrived and the customarily packed gallery

assembled to hear Ribton, with surgical precision, go through the evidence that had been presented to the Inquiry.

Before Ribton began, the chairman asked the prosecution to clarify what charge they intended to proceed with against the accused. Was she to be charged as a principal, accomplice or accessory after the fact? Mr Saunders replied that he had not been instructed to make any special application as to the form of commitment, believing that to be for the Inquiry to decide.

Ribton then kicked-off his address to the Magistrates. He, firstly, thanked the Bench for the impartiality they had shown during the investigation. Ribton ventured his belief that the main thing that had come out of the, somewhat protracted, Inquiry was that they were no closer to discovering the truth than they had been immediately after the dreadful crime had been committed.

The lawyer next attempted to debunk some of the points Mr Saunders had raised during the Inquiry. The time when the murder was committed had nothing to do with the prisoner, as the question of time could no more affect her than it could any other person who could be charged with the crime. The question of whether wounds had been committed after the death of the child again had no bearing on the case against the prisoner. The fact the dog had not been heard barking, of which much had been made, was of no importance. It had, in fact, been shown that the dog had been enclosed in the yard and that it was quite possible for someone to have bypassed it unseen.

Saunders had claimed it was impossible for someone to have been secreted inside the house, but the fact was there were several unoccupied rooms. Curiously, Superintendent Woolfe had not been directed into any of these rooms when he first examined the house.

Mr Kent himself had stated that a discharged servant had left his house vowing vengeance upon the children. Kent had also, initially, believed the child had been 'stolen'. Ribton suggested there was every possibility the original intention may have been to abduct the child. No blood traces had been found, no weapon had been discovered and no household knives were missing. Two nailed boot marks had been left on the drawing-room carpet, pointing in the direction of the window.

Ribton explained that he did not, necessarily, wish to imply the crime had been committed by a stranger, but he pointed out that such a conclusion would not be entirely inconsistent with the evidence presented.

Another speculation in which Ribton believed Saunders had indulged, was that there must have been more than one person involved. Was it so inconceivable one strong and active person could have taken a child of just under four years of age from his cot, after first stifling his cries?

Ribton then opined that the evidence presented against Constance Kent had been considerably stronger than the evidence against Elizabeth Gough. He noted the case against Constance had, correctly in his view, been dismissed. Perhaps getting slightly carried away, Ribton went on to compare the investigation carried out by Mr Slack to that of a Grand Inquisitor. The use of the rack and physical torture, he claimed, had been replaced by the mental torture Slack had applied to the witnesses called before him.

Next, Ribton pointed to the fact that when Mr Kent and his family were questioned by Slack, they'd had an attorney present to represent them, an attorney who not only put questions but interposed to prevent other questions being put. Slack had taken statements from every inmate of the house, had collated and compared them and had then drawn conclusions as to some contradictory statements that may have been made by the prisoner. What he had not done, at any stage, was to interview Elizabeth Gough and give her the opportunity to clear up any anomalies. Ribton put it to the Magistrates that the only conclusion that could be drawn was that there had been a preconceived determination to make a victim out of someone and the Inquiry had been instituted, not to uncover the truth, but to collect evidence against one individual.

The lawyer finished by stating that whilst he was not attempting to cast suspicion on any individual, he could not help but think that far stronger cases could, for example, be made against Mr Kent or Constance Kent. He trusted that the Magistrates, who had, most justly in his view, dismissed the case against Constance, would not hesitate to do the same with respect to his own unfortunate client.

The Magistrates withdrew for around thirty minutes to deliberate in private. On their return, they, not surprisingly, felt it was their duty to defend the conduct of Mr Slack during his investigations. Ribton spoke up to clarify that it had not been his intention to offend Mr Slack and said he felt sure Slack had carried out the duties assigned to him with due ability and discretion.

Elizabeth Gough was formally discharged after a relative put up a verbal bond to produce her, if required, under penalty of one hundred pounds.

It was now open season on everyone involved in the case and the press, as well as having their own thoughts on the murder, were bombarded with suggestions from the public.

Some newspapers expressed the view that it was time to move beyond normal lines of investigation. They believed it was now time to enlist help from 'the other side' by employing the services of a clairvoyant, a process still thought to be a credible method of shedding light on such mysteries at that time.

By early November, the Wiltshire police had received over two hundred anonymous letters regarding the case and the notoriety of the murder had spread throughout Europe. Yet another Inquiry was set up, this time a non-judicial one held at the Temperance Hall by local Magistrates. During this Inquiry, which dragged on for well over a week, a startling new fact arose regarding the now almost legendary missing nightdress that had so vexed Inspector Whicher of Scotland Yard.

It transpired that Sergeant Watts of the Somerset Constabulary had, on the day the murder was discovered, found a woman's chemise, stained with blood, hidden in the boiler hole of one of the kitchens in Road Hill House. Watts had handed the garment to Superintendent Foley who, following consultation with the surgeon Mr Stapleton, had concluded that the blood had been produced by natural causes and had nothing to do with the case. The chemise had subsequently disappeared.

Since then, the police had kept the matter secret, because Foley had been embarrassed by the way the situation had been handled. The Superintendent was clinging to the conviction the garment was not connected to the crime.

The Magistrates were furious with Foley and the fact it had taken five months for this information to be brought forward. It was staggering that the circumstances of the finding of the garment had been withheld from Inspector

Whicher during his own investigations. A special meeting was held on 30 November, at the Police Court in Trowbridge, to take evidence in public regarding the blood-stained item of clothing. It was thought desirable to bring the matter into the public domain.

After several witness statements were taken, the conclusion of the meeting was that the garment had no connection to the murder. Whilst there was a slap on the wrist for Foley, the meeting accepted he had acted through a sense of delicacy and decency rather than any neglect of duty.

The year of 1860 bowed out with its head hung low as the sheer incompetence of the initial local investigation into the murder of little Francis Saville Kent was laid bare.

Although the case was never far from the thoughts of the press and public, with all prospects of a further Inquiry having been exhausted the crime looked destined to become one of Britain's great unsolved mysteries.

That was to remain the position until 25 April 1865, the day Constance Emily Kent, now aged twenty-one, voluntarily surrendered herself to the Bow Street Magistrate, Sir Thomas Henry, and confessed to the murder of her half-brother. Sir Thomas did not have jurisdiction over the case so he made immediate arrangements to pass the matter to the Wiltshire Magistrates for investigation. The only detail released at this stage was that Constance Kent had declared she, and she alone, had been responsible for the murder.

Interest in the case quickly returned to fever-pitch level. The story soon hogged the headlines again and it took a momentous event to temporarily displace it, the arrival of news from the United States of America of the assassination of their President, Abraham Lincoln.

Information began to leak as to the course the life of Constance Kent had taken since her release from custody. It was revealed that following a period enrolled at a convent in France, Constance had joined a society of religious ladies in Brighton in 1863. Two years later, under no pressure to do so, she had confessed to clergyman Reverend Arthur Wagner.

On 4 May 1865, when the doors opened for the start of the examination of Constance Kent before the Wiltshire magistrates at Trowbridge, the Courthouse was besieged by the press and public, with many unable to gain admission. No attorney had been engaged for the prosecution, which was led by Inspector Williamson of Scotland Yard. Roland Rodway, an attorney from Trowbridge, watched the case on behalf of the Kent family.

Several familiar witnesses were called to recount their testimony from all these years ago. Elizabeth Gough, Thomas Berger, Joshua Parsons, Sarah Rogers (nee Cox), Esther Holly and her daughter Martha, Police Sergeant James Watts and retired Police Inspector Jonathan Whicher.

The first new witness to be called was Catherine Ann Greame, Lady Superior of St Mary's Hospital, Brighton. Ms Greame informed the Magistrates she had first met Constance Kent in August of 1863. The Lady Superior declared she had never even discussed the Road murder with Constance. She had been shocked when she heard the girl had confessed to Mr Wagner and expressed her desire to give herself up to justice.

Following the confession, Ms Greame had asked Constance if she was fully aware of the consequences of admitting to the murder and the girl had replied that she was. The Lady Superior told the Inquiry she had continued to counsel Constance on religious matters over the course of the week following the confession. During one such conversation, Constance had unexpectedly opened up to her and revealed some of the details of her actions on the night of the murder.

Ms Greame revealed Constance had told her that on the night in question, she had carried the child downstairs whilst he was still sleeping. She had then left the house through the drawing room window and made her way to the privy, where she knew she would not be disturbed. There, she had used a razor she had earlier removed from her father's dressing-case to kill the child.

Constance admitted she had removed her nightdress from the laundry basket. Believing she may have failed in an earlier attempt to clean the garment herself, Constance had panicked and retrieved the nightdress before burning it. As to motive, Constance told the Lady Superior she had borne no malice towards the child but had wished to extract some form of revenge on her stepmother for a perceived mistreatment.

Reverend Arthur Douglas Wagner, perpetual curate of St Paul's Church, Brighton, was next to be called. Wagner began by declaring that all the communications he'd had with Constance Kent were under the seal of confession and he would decline to answer any questions that would involve a breach of confidence.

The chairman reminded the Reverend of his oath, to tell the truth, the whole truth and nothing but the truth during the Inquiry. Wagner responded by saying his duty to God forbade him from divulging any information he had received during the act of confession. He would only reveal that Constance had authorised him to contact Sir George Grey, the Home Secretary, to inform him she was guilty of the

Road murder and she wished to give herself up to justice. Wagner was not prepared to say anything further, but he did clarify the girl's decision to give herself up was an entirely voluntary act.

No further questions were put to Reverend Wagner. Constance Kent was committed for trial at the next Wiltshire assizes and was then led from the dock and conveyed to Salisbury Jail. As the crowds spilt back onto the street, a small group followed the lone figure of Elizabeth Gough as she walked off into the fading evening light.

It wasn't long before Reverend Wagner felt moved to defend himself and the Lady Superior against charges in the press that he had committed the offence of betraying Constance Kent's sacramental confession. Having done his best to defend his actions on that front, Wagner then came under attack for hiding behind the sacramental confession during the Inquiry. A bit of a 'no win' situation for Reverend Wagner.

The matter was raised in Parliament and it was declared that the law of the country did not recognise any privilege by which a clergyman was entitled to withhold evidence in courts of law which may be material to the interests of Justice. Sir George Grey made it clear that during the formal trial of Constance Kent, should Reverend Wagner, if called, refuse to answer any proper question put to him, it would be for the presiding Judge to deal with him as he would with any other witness who refused to give evidence essential to the ends of justice.

The trial of Constance Kent, before Judge Willes, finally took place on 21 July 1865. Mr Karslake and Mr Lopes led the prosecution, Mr Coleridge, Mr Edlin and Mr Ravenhill appeared for the defence. Constance, in a barely audible voice, pleaded guilty to the charge of having wilfully and intentionally murdered her half-brother. Mr Coleridge then addressed the Court to make a statement on behalf of his client.

Coleridge informed the Court that Constance, as a person who valued her own soul, wished him to make clear the guilt was hers alone and her father and the others who had suffered by being under suspicion were entirely innocent. He then said that the young woman had also asked him to convey to the Court that she had not been driven to the act by any unkind treatment she had received in her home. Unfortunately, the actual reason why Constance had committed the brutal crime was missing from the statement.

Satisfied Constance had been granted full access to the advice of her defence counsel, the Judge accepted her plea of guilty to the charge. After donning the dreaded black cap, Judge Willes imposed the only sentence available to him, the death sentence.

The Judge then pointed out that it was the prerogative of the Queen to show mercy. He offered that Kent's youth at the time of the murder, together with the fact she had voluntary confessed, may be taken into consideration. He also made it clear, however, that it was not his position to make assumptions as to Her Majesty's thoughts on the matter.

Constance Kent, her face concealed under the cover of a black veil, was duly led from the dock to face her fate.

On 22 August 1865, Queen Victoria commuted the sentence of death that had been passed on Constance Kent to one of penal servitude for life. Kent would go on to serve just twenty years in jail before being released. In 1886, she emigrated from Britain to Australia, where she joined her brother William. Changing her name to Ruth Emilie Kaye, she worked as a nurse until her retirement in 1932.

On 10 April 1944, Constance Kent died aged 100. If anyone else had been involved in the murder, their secret was cremated along with the body of Constance Kent in Rookwood Necropolis, Sydney.

The potential powder-keg regarding the refusal of Reverend Wagner to disclose information arising from sacramental confession was never ignited. Thanks to the acceptance of Kent's confession in court, Wagner was not called on to testify. The controversy the matter had stirred did, however, rumble on for several years.

Former Police Inspector Whicher was fully vindicated. The press attempted to go some way towards making amends for the treatment he had received at their hands by publishing, in full, a letter Whicher had written to the Chief Superintendent of the Bristol Police five years earlier, dated 23 November 1860:-

'Road Murder,

I am addressing a few lines to you relative to the above case, as I have not had the pleasure of seeing you since the discharge of Miss Constance, for whose arrest I had such castigation from all quarters.

Although I admit there was not sufficient evidence for her further detention, still I believe, had there been counsel for the prosecution to have opened the case and examined the witnesses properly, it would have assumed a somewhat different shape in public opinion. The witness, Miss Moody, in reference to *animus*, did not give the evidence I was led to understand she could have done.

Regarding the nightdress taken from the clothes-basket two days after the murder, it was no part of my theory that it was the one worn on the night of the murder, but the one put on afterwards, slept in for the remainder of the night and found in the morning by Superintendent Foley and Mr Parsons, the surgeon. The latter described it as being very clean and says he drew Foley's attention to the fact, but it appears he did not take the hint, that it had been changed during the night. This was the dress abstracted from the clothes-basket, entered in the washing-book to the laundress, not with the view of destroying it, but of taking it back into use, to have two in possession and to make the laundress blameable for the one that was deficient.

After all that has been said about this case and the different theories advanced, there is, in my humble judgement, but one solution to it. If you had made the personal investigations I did, I am certain you would have come to the same conclusion. But possibly you, like others, have entirely been led by what you have heard, especially about the theory of Mr Kent and the nurse being concerned in the murder, simply upon the vague suspicion that he might have been in her room.

In my opinion, if there ever was one man more to be pitied, or who has been more calumniated than another, that unfortunate man is Mr Kent. It was bad enough to have his darling child cruelly murdered, but to be branded as the murderer is far worse. According to the present state of public opinion, he will be so branded to the day of his death unless a confession is made by the person who I, firmly, believe committed the deed. I have little doubt that confession would have been made if Miss Constance had been remanded for another week.

I believe, in the first place, the fact of there being two families, or rather a stepmother and a family by that stepmother, was the primal cause of the murder and the motive was jealousy towards the children by the second marriage. The deceased was the favourite child and spite towards the parents, particularly the mother, I believe to have been the actuating motive of Constance Kent.

The reasons for my suspicions are as follows:-

Miss Constance possesses an extraordinary mind, which I think is proved by what she and her brother did on a former occasion. The two medical men mixed up in the present case believe her to be a monomaniac. Nothing happens to the child while she is at school, but on the fourteenth night after her arrival in the house, the child is murdered, by someone in the house. Who was there in that house likely to entertain any bad feeling towards the deceased but the person in question?

Whoever did the deed no doubt did it in their nightclothes. When Constance Kent went to bed that night she had three nightdresses belonging to her in the house. After the murder, she had but two. What, then, became of the third? It was not lost in the wash, as it was so craftily endeavoured to make it appear, but it was got rid of in some other way. Where is it and what became of it? I do not think the knife was intended to have been used in the first place, but the wicked plan was to have thrown the poor child down the privy, believing he would have sunk into the soil out of sight.

The window was probably opened before the murder, thereby intending to make it appear the child had been stolen. When it was found the child would not pass down the privy, the knife was used with a view to making death certain. That is my theory and if a more reasonable one can be adduced I will most willingly bow to it, but until then I cannot alter it, although I am aware it is not the prevailing one.

I want to draw your particular attention to a most important fact that oozed out the other day at Mr Saunders' Inquiry, which was stifled in its birth by the police concerned, or at least they attempted to do so by pooh-poohing it. It now appears that on the day of the murder, on searching the house, the police found a bloodstained nightshift secreted in the boiler-hole in the back kitchen.

Up to the time of Saunders' Inquiry, this all-important fact had been kept a perfect secret and would not have come out had it not been for a Sergeant Watts, of the Somerset Constabulary, letting it out in some way. He does not appear to have been compromised in the losing of it.

I see the matter was passed over very lightly by Foley and Dallimore, of the Wiltshire police, telling Saunders they did not take the trouble to find out who it belonged to as they had shown it to the surgeon, Mr Stapleton, who said the stains arose from natural causes. They put it back in the boiler-hole again, or down the side of it, and that was all they knew about it.

Regarding their having shown the dress to Mr Stapleton, it turns out to be an untruth, as the one they showed him was one belonging to the elder Miss Kent, which was found in her bedroom. Mr Stapleton says they never showed him the one found in the boiler-hole, nor did they ever name the circumstances to me or to any of the Magistrates.

The truth of the matter is, I have no doubt, that by some carelessness they lost possession of it, either by putting it out of their hands and Constance got possession of it again, or they put it back in the boiler-hole to try and catch the owner coming to take it away. It having been got away without their knowledge, a compact of secrecy was entered into, which was well kept, for, as I said before, not one word was said to me or the Magistrates, or in fact to anyone, about the finding of this dress, or shift. It would not have come out now if it had not been for Watts, who found it but was not compromised in the losing of it.

Where it was must now, through this bungling, like the other part of the case, remain a mystery. The Magistrates are making an investigation into the matter and I am told that on finding the statement that the dress was shown to Mr Stapleton was denied by him, the police said it had been found to belong to the cook. On inquiry, this also turns out to be untrue.

Just imagine a bloodstained garment being found in a house where a murder has just been committed. Supposing the account first given to be true, to put it back into the hiding place again, without further inquiry, would hardly be believed. I have, however, little doubt it was let slip in the way I have described and that would account for what I could never get an explanation for, why the men were secreted in the kitchen the same night. Foley never would explain that to me, but Mr Kent said in his evidence that Foley told him it was to see if anyone got up to destroy anything, but they did not tell him what they had found.'

The 'former occasion' involving Constance, to which Whicher referred in his letter, related to an incident some four years prior to the murder. Constance had gone to the same outdoor privy in which the child's dead body would later be discovered, to crop her hair and change into boy's clothes before running away from home, accompanied by her brother, William.

Although it's possible Whicher had not got every detail of the crime correct, it seems clear the case would have been solved if anything resembling proper police procedures had been followed during the initial investigation. It should have been obvious from the first that the crime had been committed by someone from within the household. It, therefore, should have been relatively easy to seal off the crime scene, which would surely have helped prevent the disappearance of vital evidence. The deference of the investigators towards the family led to crucial delays in interviewing and searching all the potential witnesses and suspects.

One of the many lessons to be learned was that everyone in the household should have been questioned without fear or favour. At the time, such investigations were driven by local Magistrates and it was possible for the local police to be heavily influenced by the social status of those under investigation. The attention attracted by this case would bring into focus the inadequacies of such an approach.

Whilst the arrival on the scene of Scotland Yard at least resulted in a proper investigation eventually being carried out, the damage had already been done. It must be admitted that given the lack of any material evidence, it was always going to take a confession to close the case.

3 DALSTON GOES BALLISTIC

Dalston is a district of north-east London, located in the Borough of Hackney.

Police-Constable George Cole was a young, recently married policeman who had previously served six years in the 46th Regiment of the British Army before following a well-trodden path into the police force. It was around 9:30pm on 1 December 1882 when Cole, dressed in uniform and wrapped in a great coat that offered some protection from the foul night air, left home to begin his night's duty.

It would not have come as any surprise to Cole that the streets of his beat in Dalston were shrouded in the thick, dank, low-hanging fog for which London had become renowned. Under the cover of that same all-encompassing blanket of fog, local east-end petty criminal Thomas Orrock was just setting off to carry out his maiden burglary.

In a bid to raise his low-ranked criminal underworld profile among his unsavoury group of friends, Orrock had recently answered an advertisement for a 'revolver for sale' in the Exchange and Mart. The advert had read, 'New pocket revolver, nickel, pin-fire, spring-acting, in Japan case, with 25 cartridges, price 10s 6d, a bargain; J Maclellan, 21 Vicarage Road, Tottenham, London'.

Orrock had duly arrived at the house in Vicarage Road, armed only with a copy of the advert, where he was greeted by the occupants, Jose Maclellan and his wife, May Ann. After a brief bout of bartering, Orrock agreed to pay 10/- for the pistol and ammunition.

Thomas Orrock decided to select a suitably soft option for his 'breakthrough crime' and targeted the local Baptist Chapel in Dalston. It was a place well enough known to Orrock, who had been born into a respectable and highly religious family and was a member of the chapel's congregation. A cabinet-maker by trade, the would-be burglar had no trouble putting together a selection of tools for the robbery. The 'tool' he would later live to regret taking along was the pocket revolver.

Orrock, draped in dark clothing and wearing a black soft felt hat, was standing beneath a lamppost close to the door of the Baptist Chapel, when he was spotted by Police-Constable Frederick Cobb, of N Division. Cobb, who was just coming to the end of his night's duty, commented to his fellow officer, Police-Constable Brockwell, on the man lurking under the ghostly glow of light emitting from the lamp as it penetrated through the dank mist. Having no reason to suspect the man of any wrongdoing, the police officers moved on, walking past the chapel to the nearby police station to end their shift. Cobb subsequently made his way home for a well-earned rest.

After the two policemen had moved away, Orrock, while his nerve held, decided to make his move and stepped over to the chapel. He selected a low window and was in the process of forcing it open when he was startled by the approach of yet another policeman, George Cole. The policeman quickly grabbed hold of Orrock's sleeve and during the brief struggle that ensued, the chisel the would-be burglar had been using to force the window open fell to the ground.

Cole managed to get a firm grip of Orrock's arm and began to direct him towards the nearby police station. Orrock, however, had no intention of going quietly and used his free hand to reach into his pocket, where his fingers fell upon his recently purchased revolver. Without pausing to think of the consequences, Orrock fired three wild shots at the policeman. One shot struck Cole's truncheon case whilst another hit the policeman in the head, just behind his right ear. Cole bravely, but vainly, tried to hold onto his prisoner, but the man slid from his faltering grip.

As he lay wounded on the chapel steps, Cole watched Orrock slinking off into the mist. The constable made one last valiant attempt to pursue the fleeing man, but, as the life began to drain from him, he stumbled in the chapel's carriageway and slumped down into the gutter.

The sound of the shots had penetrated through the night air and two policemen, Constables Hart and Harford, rushed to the scene from their routine patrol in Dalston Lane. A group of people were already gathering nearby when the two policemen arrived, but they pushed through and saw George Cole lying in a pool of his own blood. Hart left Harford to attend to the wounded officer while he ran down the streets surrounding the chapel in the hope of gaining sight of the shooter.

Having had no success, Hart returned to the scene of the shooting. Police-Constable Cole was very weak, but still alive. Arrangements were hastily made to convey the stricken policeman to German Hospital, in Dalston Place. German Hospital had, initially, been set up to offer free treatment to the German-speaking immigrants who worked and lived in the poor conditions in the east-end of London. It also cared for English-speakers in cases of emergency and most of its out-patients were the English-speaking poor from the surrounding area.

Unfortunately, within five minutes of his arrival at the

hospital, Constable George Cole was pronounced dead. A later post-mortem would reveal a pistol-shot wound to the policeman's head, just behind his left ear. The bullet had penetrated the skull and lodged in the brain. A second wound, to the back of the head, had fractured the skull and had likely been caused when Cole had fallen to the pavement. The bullet was removed and held as evidence and the cause of death was declared as having been the result of a pistol-shot wound.

A search of the murder scene was quickly organised by Inspector Hammond of N Division. Hammond found a black felt hat on the roadway in Ashwin Street, about twelve yards from where Constable Cole's fatally wounded body had lain.

A low wall ran in front of the Baptist Chapel. Beyond the wall lay a low window offering easy access to the chapel. It was between the wall and the window that Constable Harford discovered two chisels and a wedge.

Police-Constable Cobb was interviewed and provided a description of the man he had seen loitering in the area earlier that night. The man was described as, 'about twenty-one-years-old, five-foot-two-inches tall, pale complexion, round-faced, wearing a dark soft felt hat, dressed in a long dark overcoat and light trousers'.

Police carried out a thorough examination of Constable Cole's belongings and Police-Constable Brockwell noticed a small hole in the fallen officer's truncheon case. Brockwell removed the truncheon and saw it had a small indentation directly in line with the hole in the case. As he lifted the truncheon case to take a closer look at the hole, a small bullet fell out.

Interviews took place with the members of the public that had gathered at the scene of the shooting and police discovered there were two women that had witnessed the incident.

Elizabeth Ann Shepherd, who resided at 3 Ashwin Street, ran the refreshment rooms at nearby Dalston Station. Shepherd had just been leaving her home to head towards the station when she had seen two men struggling in the roadway, directly opposite her house. She had not been able to make out the faces of the two men, but she had recognised one was dressed in a police uniform. As she was locking the door of the house, she had heard a gunshot, quickly followed by another. The startled woman had then rushed back to unlock her door and retreat to the safety of her home. As she did so, she had heard the policeman cry out for help. Unfortunately, Shepherd was unable to provide a useful description of the other man she had seen involved in the struggle, other than that he had been wearing a wide-awake hat on his head.

Elizabeth Bucknell, a local resident in Reeve's Cottages, had been on her way back from the Crown and Castle Pub, where she had dutifully collected some beer for her father when she spotted a policeman and another man struggling in the middle of the road. The policeman had taken hold of the man's collar and as the man started to resist the two men had stumbled back toward the Baptist Chapel. The men had kept up the struggle until they were just outside number three Ashwin Street and it was then that Bucknell had heard the first gunshot. The struggle had continued and Bucknell had heard the second shot as the two men reached the chapel. The policeman had then slumped to the ground and called out for help, which had prompted the woman to run into Dalston Lane to seek assistance. Bucknell had not spotted any other witnesses in the vicinity but she ran straight into two policemen who were rushing to the scene. It was just then that she had heard a further gunshot.

Bucknell claimed to have managed to get a good look at the shooter and described him as being about five-foot-two-inches tall, aged about twenty-two or twenty-three, wearing a long dark overcoat, a light pair of trousers and a black felt hat.

Robert Bucknell, Elizabeth's father, had been alerted by the commotion outside his house and as he opened his front door he was greeted by the sight of a young man, dressed in dark coat and light trousers, rushing by and heading towards Abbot Street.

Having been provided with a reasonable description of the man they were seeking and with several people having witnessed the shooting, police were confident of a quick arrest. Their confidence was sadly misplaced.

The Home Secretary, justifiably outraged by the killing of a policeman, quickly ordered that a reward of two hundred pounds be offered for any information leading to the apprehension of the murderer. All local householders were asked to advise the police of any suspicious circumstances surrounding lodgers in their homes, particularly any that had been seen wearing the type of hat discovered at the crime scene.

In the meantime, Thomas Orrock had slipped back into his life as a respectable cabinet-maker and regular church attendee. It is believed he attended the funeral of Police-Constable Cole. A few weeks later he married a young lady who was a member of the congregation of the very church he had sought to rob on the day of the policeman's murder.

As the days passed, it began to appear to the public that the investigation into Police-Constable Cole's murder had stalled. Behind the scenes, however, a small group of dedicated police officers were piecing together the clues that would eventually lead to the capture of the murderer of their fallen colleague.

One of the chisels recovered from the crime scene bore faded letters which had been crudely scratched onto the tool and appeared to spell out 'r-o-c-k'. It was clear other letters that had, at one time, preceded these had faded beyond recognition.

Matters were to take a fortuitous turn, at least as far as the police were concerned, when cabinet-maker Thomas Orrock was arrested on an entirely unrelated charge for a burglary around six months after his botched attempt to rob the Baptist Chapel. Clearly, Orrock was not cut out for the robbery business.

Orrock's cabinet-making background, together with the link to the letters scratched onto the chisel recovered at the crime scene, aroused the suspicion of the Dalston policemen, who were still working determinedly to catch Police-Constable Cole's killer. Elizabeth Ann Shepherd and Elizabeth Bucknell were taken to Clerkenwell Prison, where Orrock was being held, but neither woman could pick him out from an identity parade.

Orrock was found guilty of burglary and incarcerated in Coldbath Fields Prison.

On 1 February 1884, Police-Constable Cobb was taken to the prison and picked out Orrock as the man he had seen on the night of the murder of Constable Cole, though even this was at the second attempt as he had picked out another man the first time around, before changing his mind as the line-up was being led out.

For the moment, Orrock was still in the clear as the dogged policemen continued to seek the evidence that would provide them with a strong enough case to bring a charge of murder against him. They began checking into Orrock's background and managed to track down two of his less than savoury friends, Frederick Miles and Arthur Evans, both of whom were found to have been in Orrock's company on the day of the murder. Indeed, it transpired that Miles had been at the actual crime scene that night and had volunteered to run and fetch a doctor after the shooting had occurred. The testimony of these two men and another of Orrick's friends, Henry Mortimer, would prove to be crucial in cracking the case.

During his interrogation of Frederick Miles, Police-Constable Cobb learned Orrock had been practising with a revolver shortly before the night of the murder. The policeman arranged for Miles to accompany him to Tottenham Marshes, where Miles pointed out a tree, halfway between the Ferry Boat public-house and the railway bridge that crossed over the River Lea. Cobb examined the tree and used a chisel to remove several bullets from it.

After matching the bullets taken from the tree with those taken from the body and truncheon case of Constable Cole, the police finally brought a charge against Thomas Henry Orrock for the murder of Police-Constable George Cole.

On 21 August 1884, Thomas Orrock, described as a cabinet-maker, was brought from Coldbath Fields Prison, where he was serving a twelve-month sentence for burglary, to the Police Court in Bow Street. There he would stand before Sir James Ingham on a charge of the wilful murder of George

Cole, a constable of the N Division of the Metropolitan Police. Mr Poland, instructed by Mr Pollard, appeared for the prosecution and Mr Willis led the defence.

Poland began by outlining the events that had occurred on the night of the policeman's death. He then said two witnesses had described the perpetrator as being a young man with a sallow complexion and a slight moustache, dressed in a long dark coat with light trousers and wearing a black felt wide-awake hat. Following a search of the murder scene, police had discovered two chisels, a small wooden wedge and a black wide-awake hat.

One of the chisels, Poland revealed, was seen to have scratches on it. Evidently, an attempt had been made to obliterate something etched into the tool. Following a microscopic examination, the letters 'r-o-c-k' had been identified. An enlarged photograph of the chisel had then been taken.

Poland outlined how, after Orrock had been arrested on a separate burglary charge, the police had received information leading them to believe he was the man seen struggling with Police-Constable Cole on the night of the policeman's murder. Enquiries had then been made regarding known associates of Thomas Orrock and police had tracked down two men who would be called to testify for the prosecution, Frederick Miles and Arthur Evans. Miles had been positively identified as having been at the crime scene on the night of the shooting, where he had offered to procure medical assistance for the stricken policeman.

Before Miles and Evans testified, the three main witnesses to the shooting were called, Eliza Shepherd, Elizabeth Bucknell and Robert Bucknell. Though all three had been able to provide the police with some description of the man they had seen struggling with the policeman and were able to describe what the man had been wearing, none of them had been able to positively identify Thomas Orrock as having been that man.

Police-Constable Hart and Inspector Hammond were next up and they described their arrival at the shooting scene and the discovery of the tools and the black felt hat.

The room then fell silent as the Court heard from the deeply affected widow, Elizabeth Cole. Mrs Cole told how, on the night of 1 December 1882, her husband had left their house at 9:30pm to begin his duty and she had not seen him again until she had been shown his lifeless body in the German Hospital.

The next witness to be called was the sister of the accused, Mrs Beere, who recalled how, on the night of 1 December 1882, her brother had returned to their home, in Bagstow Road, Stoke Newington, between 10 and 11pm. Orrock, who had been wearing a long black coat and light coloured trousers, had gone directly to his bedroom. When the witness saw him a short time later, she noticed he had a small tear in one of the knees of his trousers and asked him how this had happened. Orrock had told her he had been involved in a fight but would say no more before retiring to bed.

A few days later, Mrs Beere had mended the torn trousers and a tear on the sleeve of the prisoner's overcoat. She was not aware at the time that her brother's black felt hat was missing. The witness was unable to identify the hat produced in Court as belonging to her brother.

Beere went on to describe her brother as being a regular attendee at services and bible classes at the Baptist Chapel and revealed that he had married a young lady, who was also a member of the congregation, shortly after the night of the policeman's death. She then stated that her brother was a cabinet-maker by trade, working at Mr Pottinger's.

A fellow cabinet-maker at Pottinger's, Arthur Evans, was then called and was asked to give an account of his recollections of events on the night of the policeman's death. Evans revealed that he had been in the company of the prisoner and another man, Frederick Miles, in a public-house called the London Apprentice during the hours of 12 to 1pm on the day in question.

Later that day, the three men had met up again, between 6 and 7pm, at the Star and Garter public-house before moving on to the Walford Pub, where they had stayed until 8pm. Inside the Star and Garter, Orrock had shown the men some chisels which he claimed to have had returned from the grinders. Inside the Walford, Evans had noticed Orrock was in possession of a pistol and had asked why. Orrock replied that he was carrying it 'in case anyone interfered with him'.

As the drinking continued and tongues began to loosen, Orrock had revealed his intention to use the chisels to break into the Baptist Chapel. Shortly thereafter, Evans had been left behind as Orrock and Miles disappeared from the pub before returning about forty-five minutes later. The three men then moved from the Walford back to the Star and Garter, where they consumed a pot of ale before moving on to the Railway Tavern, passing the Chapel on the way.

Inside the Railway Tavern, Orrock had expanded on his plan to break into the Chapel and had said he intended to climb over the gates of the public-house, which adjoining the Chapel, then planned to steal the sacramental plate. His intention was to then take the plate to his brother-in-law, Mr Tilley, to have it melted down. Orrock left the pub and attempted to unfasten one of the Chapel windows but returned shortly afterwards, claiming there were too many people milling about to proceed with the break-in.

As the three men circled back to the Star and Garter for a beer top-up, Orrock declared he would now require a lamp, so they stopped off at a nearby lamp-shop, where a suitable item was purchased for seven pence.

By around 10pm, enough beer had been consumed to provide Orrock with the courage to push ahead with his master-plan, though by this time he had changed his proposed point of entry to a window in a recess behind a low wall in Ashwin Street. Evans and Miles had headed back into the Railway Tavern while Orrock veered off towards the Chapel.

Evans claimed to have heard three fog signals going off from his seat within the pub, but, when pressed by Poland, he then admitted he had, in fact, thought the reports were those of a firearm. On hearing the gunshots, Evans and Miles had run out of the pub, where they were greeted by a cry for help coming from somewhere within the swirling mist that had descended upon the surrounding streets.

Evans had then decided to quickly head for home but, as he passed the Chapel, he came upon the wounded policeman and the police colleagues who were attending to him. Shortly thereafter, the police had carried the wounded man away. Following a nerve-steadying drink in yet another pub, Evans had finally made his way home to his place of residence in Tottenham.

The witness was asked by Poland to confirm whether the hat produced in Court had belonged to Orrock. Evans said he believed it had and stated he had tried on the hat himself on the night in question. He went on to describe Orrock as having been wearing the hat together with a long black overcoat and light coloured trousers, though he said Orrock had no moustache at the time.

Evans said he had next met up with Orrock in the Adam and Eve public-house, where the subject of the reward of two hundred pounds on offer for information leading to the capture of the policeman's murderer had been raised. Orrock had asked him if he was looking to get his hands on the reward and Evans had replied, 'No, I would not put you away for a thousand pounds.' Orrock had then told the witness that Miles had taken an oath that if one of the others informed, then their 'lights should be put out'. Evans was asked to swear the same oath, which he duly did.

The next time the two men had met was on a tramcar a week or so later, when Orrock had informed Evans he had attended the policeman's burial.

When pressed by Poland on whether Orrock had provided any details of what had occurred on the night of the shooting, there was an agonising delay before Evans responded. When he finally spoke, Evans said Orrock had told him that if the policemen had taken him quietly and had not struggled for the revolver, he would not have been shot. The policeman had discovered Orrock at the chapel window and had asked what he was doing. Evans continued, stating that Orrock had claimed to have thrown the pistol away. The policeman had then 'had a go for it' and in the ensuing struggle, he'd been shot. Orrock had then told the witness he had picked up the revolver and ran home, unaware he had left his hat behind.

Evans claimed to have never seen the pistol before the night in the pub and said he had not seen Orrock wearing the long black coat, the soft felt hat or the light-coloured trousers after the night of the shooting. At this stage, Mr Willis reserved his cross-examination of the witness.

Detective-Sergeant Brockwell and the recently promoted Sergeant Cobb then provided their evidence to the Court, before proceedings were halted for the day and the prisoner was remanded.

On the resumption of proceedings, Augustus Wilson, a photographer based in Dalston Lane, was called on to recount the events of the day Sergeant Cobb had handed a chisel to him and had asked him to produce an enlarged photograph of it. Wilson had examined the chisel before taking the photograph and he confirmed it was the same chisel produced in the courtroom. In the enlarged photograph, the scratches on the chisel had been shown to reveal the letters 'r-o-c-k'.

James Cameron, a Fellow of the Institute of Chemistry, who had been engaged in a laboratory in Somerset House, was next to be called. Cameron told the Court he had been visited by Inspector Glass. At the Inspector's request, Cameron had examined a chisel under a powerful microscope and had been able to make out two words, one of which had been superimposed over the other. The uppermost word spelt 'r-o-c-k'. The word beneath appeared to read 'O-r-r-o-c-k', though some of the letters were imperfect. In Cameron's opinion, the word 'O-r-r-o-c-k' had been overwritten with the word 'r-o-c-k' and some of the strokes in the uppermost name had cut through some of those in the lower name. This, in Cameron's view, was made quite evident with the use of a strong microscope.

Next to be called was Thomas Jones, an employee at Salisbury's lamp-dealers, who testified as to having checked his records at the request of the police. The records had confirmed he had sold a lamp at around 9pm on the night of the shooting, though Jones was not able to identify the man to whom he had sold the lamp.

The next witness to be called was altogether more important, Frederick Miles, who gave his own account of the pub-crawl that led to him meeting up with Orrock and Evans in the Walford Pub on the night of 1 December 1882.

Orrock had asked the witness what his plans were for that night. On hearing Miles had nothing planned, Orrock had then asked him to come along to the Baptist Chapel 'to fetch some plate'. According to Miles, the prisoner had not asked him to assist in the robbery but wanted his assistance in conveying the plate to his brother-in-law's, where it could then be melted down. Promised he would receive something for his troubles, the witness had agreed to help.

The witness then described the journey via the local pubs that brought the three men to the Railway Tavern at around 10pm. Miles revealed he was aware of Orrock having the chisels in his possession, but claimed not to have witnessed the purchase of the lamp or seen the revolver that night. He had, however, seen Orrock in possession of a revolver some four months earlier.

Orrock had left the pub shortly after 10pm and Evans had gone out shortly thereafter. It was not long before the sound of gunshots was heard, though the witness claimed he initially believed them to be fog signals. The noise had been enough to bring Miles to the door of the pub, where he saw people running towards the Chapel. Miles joined the group and soon came upon the wounded policeman. Miles had recognised a constable named Ash, who was trying to assist his stricken colleague, and he'd offered to fetch a doctor but was told that the policemen were going to try to convey the man to the nearby hospital. By this time, Miles had been joined at the scene by Evans, though the witness had not seen Orrock since had left the pub.

Mr Poland showed Miles the black felt hat recovered at the crime scene and Miles confirmed his belief that the hat had belonged to Orrock. Miles recalled that during the day of the shooting, Orrock had been ribbed about being dressed like a parson, due to his long black overcoat, black hat and light trousers.

Miles then said he had not seen Orrock from the night of the shooting until his appearance in the courtroom. He had known Orrock for about ten years and was aware he had purchased a revolver after seeing an advertisement in the Exchange and Mart. Indeed, Miles had accompanied Orrock and a man named Henry Mortimer to the house in Vicarage Road where the transaction had been completed. On their return from Vicarage Road, the men had stopped off at Tottenham Marshes, where Orrock had practised using the gun by firing three or four shots into a tree. Miles claimed not to have seen the revolver since that day.

Sometime in May 1884, Miles had been approached by Sergeant Cobb and he had immediately realised what it was going to be about. Miles had cooperated with the policeman, though he had made it clear he had no interest in the reward of two hundred pounds that was on offer. At Cobb's request, Miles had led the policeman to the tree in Tottenham Marshes that Orrock had used for target practice.

Miles swore to the Court that he had never discussed the shooting with anyone before speaking to Cobb. Although he had believed Orrock may have been responsible, he had kept silent on the matter as he did not wish anyone to think he was trying to get his hands on the reward money. The witness did point out, however, that he had fully cooperated with the police as soon as he had been approached.

The next witness to be called was Charles Nelson, the deacon of the Baptist Church. The deacon revealed that Orrock, his sister and the woman he was later to marry had seats at the church and were regular attendees. On the night of the shooting, a singing practice had been held in the chapel schoolroom and this had concluded before 10pm.

Nelson then stated that twelve plated cups and twelve plates were used in the administration of the sacrament at the chapel. They were not kept on the premises, however, but were brought in for use then taken away under the charge of the secretary of the chapel. This was a fact that would not have been widely known among the chapel's congregation.

A local gunsmith from Whitechapel, James Squires, was next up. Squires had examined three bullets that had been brought to him, one recovered from the tree in Tottenham Marshes, one from the head of Constable Cole and one from the policeman's truncheon. Squires had identified all three as being pin-fire bullets, fired from a small Lefaucheux revolver of 7mm calibre. He identified the bullets as pin-fire as they only had one ring, central-fire and rim-fire having two.

The next two witnesses, Henry Mortimer and William Ames, who were both serving time in prison during the period of the trial, were friends of Orrock. Mortimer had met up with Orrock, Miles and Evans on the day of the shooting, but had left their company at around 5pm and had not seen them after that time. The witness had accompanied Orrock when he had purchased the revolver but claimed not to have seen it again since that day.

Mortimer said he had met Orrock a few months after the shooting and had asked him if he knew anything about the Dalston murder that was featuring in all the newspapers. He had been shocked when Orrock had replied, 'Would you be surprised to know that I did it? If I have done it and they prove it, I am willing to stand the consequences.' Mortimer then told the Court he had never discussed the matter with Miles or Evans and had not spoken of it until he was approached, in prison, by Sergeant Cobb.

William Ames deposed that he had known Orrock for about two years prior to the policeman's murder. Ames was an apprentice to Mr Pottinger, the cabinet-maker, and he identified the wedge produced in Court as being of the type typically used in the trade. He then went on to identify the chisels as having belonged to Orrock and disclosed that the prisoner would take them to Mrs Preston's to be ground. Mrs Preston was in the habit of scratching the names of the owners onto the tools and this had been done on those belonging to the accused.

Under cross-examination by Mr Willis, Ames admitted it was possible that Orrock's name could have been scratched onto another man's tools in error.

Ames had been aware Orrock owned a revolver and claimed that sometime after the shooting, the accused had told him the gun had been broken up and thrown in the river.

At the end of a long day, after hearing the testimony of some highly dubious characters, the trial was adjourned and the prisoner remanded.

When the trial resumed, Mr and Mrs Maclellan testified as to the revolver and ammunition they had sold, though they were unable to positively identify Orrock as having been the man who had purchased the items.

Yet another cabinet-maker, Richard Green, spoke next and revealed that a few days after the murder, he had been asked by Albert Pottinger Jnr to pawn two coats. One of the coats had been a long dark coat and the two coats had fetched five pounds in total from the pawnbroker. Green then recounted a conversation he'd had with Orrock during which he had raised the matter of the shooting of the policeman. Orrock had merely smiled and Green, having suspicions about the prisoner's involvement, had asked what had happened to the wide-awake hat and the pistol he had known Orrock to possess. Orrock had replied that he had lost the hat and that the revolver was where no one would find it, at the bottom of a river.

Next up was Albert Pottinger Jnr, son of the owner of the cabinet-making business at which Orrock had been employed. Pottinger confirmed that prior to the shooting of the policeman, he had seen the prisoner wearing the black felt hat which was shown to him by the Court, but he had not seen it again since that time. Pottinger then revealed that in February 1883, he had purchased a pair of light coloured trousers from Orrock. The trousers had shown signs of having been torn at the knees, but they had been neatly mended. Shortly afterwards, the witness had also purchased a long dark coat from Orrock, though he had since arranged for the coat to be pawned.

After calling on Ann Preston to identify her work on the chisel was produced in Court, Pollard declared that he and Mr Poland had concluded their case for the prosecution.

Mr Willis reserved his defence and Sir James Ingham then formally committed Orrock for trial at the Central Criminal Court.

The trial of Thomas Orrock at the Old Bailey, before Justice Hawkins, began on 19 September 1884. A packed courtroom saw Mr Poland and Mr Montague Williams conduct the prosecution and Mr Overend and Mr Forrest Fulton appear for the defence.

Poland opened by outlining the events leading to Orrock's appearance in Court, then followed up by deposing the same witnesses that had been called at the Police Court to back-up the prosecution's case.

As we have pretty much covered the prosecution case already, we shall concentrate on the defence by Mr Forrest Fulton, three of the major witness statements and the closing arguments.

The first two witnesses called were Elisa Shepherd and Elizabeth Bucknell. Under cross-examination, Mr Fulton established that the struggle Shepherd had witnessed had taken place during a foggy night and she was unable to positively identify the man who had been fighting with the policeman. He then pointed out that when Bucknell had initially given a statement to the police regarding what the man had been wearing, she had described his hat as being a hard felt hat'. The hat produced in Court was, in fact, a soft felt hat.

The policemen who provided evidence went largely unchallenged by Mr Fulton, then Arthur Evans provided his statement. Given its importance to the case, it is probably best to relay Evan's testimony in full and allow it to speak for itself:-

'I live at 37 Britannia Street, City Road, and am twenty-eight years of age. I am a cabinet-maker by trade and I have known the prisoner for between ten and twelve years by working in Pottinger's shop with him.

On Friday, 1st December 1882, I had work to go to, but I had been on the drink all the week. On the day on which the policeman was shot, I was at a public-house called the London Apprentice, between 12 and 1 o'clock. That place is by Old Street, Curtain Road. I met the prisoner there, and a young man named Frederick Miles was there, and we three were together.

I know a young man named Mortimer, at that time he was living at Coxhall Street, Bridport Place, Hoxton, and we all went in that direction. The prisoner was outside. The prisoner and Miles went away then, they returned later, I stayed there and I had about three-quarters of an hour's sleep.

I saw these chisels outside the Walford. Orrock had the 1 1/4-inch one, and I believe Miles carried the other one. Miles brought it there, but I believe Orrock carried it. Miles had it when I first saw it and he gave it to Orrock, tied up in a red handkerchief along with the 1 1/4-inch one. I did not see any wedge. There was also a 3/4 and 7/8-inch chisel, I had those. Orrock gave them to me and I gave the 3/4-inch one back to Orrock. The 3/4 and 7/8-inch ones were shown to me before the Magistrate. I never gave the 7/8-inch chisel back to Orrock, I broke it at my work.

I'm not sure whether Orrock used to have his chisels ground at Preston's, in Old Street, they were fetched from there that afternoon. I can't tell whether it was Orrock or Miles who fetched them. This broken chisel, after I broke it, I left at Pottinger's, where I had been employed. Preston's is a place where they grind tools.

I first saw the revolver which Orrock had outside the Walford. He showed it to me. It was a pin-fire revolver, you could put it in your waistcoat pocket. I had it in my hand and nearly shot him with it. I did not know before that night he had a revolver, he said he had it in case anyone interfered with him. I did not see whether it was loaded and did not see any marks.

Orrock said he was going to the chapel. That was when we were in the London Apprentice before we got to the Walford. He did not say then what he was going to do there and he did not say what chapel. We left the Walford, at about 9 o'clock, and Miles, Orrock and I went to the Star and Garter, at the corner of Ball's Pond Road and Kingsland Road, then afterwards we went to the Railway Tavern, at the corner of Ashwin Street. We got there through Abbott Street, down Beech Street, and past the chapel. As we passed the chapel, Orrock said he was going to get into the chapel to fetch the sacrament plate. He said he could smash it up and carry it out under his coat.

I noticed the room underneath the chapel was open and was being used for a meeting. The prisoner stopped to speak to a girl at the door. I waited opposite, then we three went to the Railway Tavern and met Miles there, he had gone on first. We all came out of the Railway Tavern and went to the Star and Garter and had a drop more beer. Orrock then said, 'I must have a lamp on the job', so we went to a lamp shop in High Street, Kingsland. I believe the prisoner went in. I, shortly afterwards, saw Orrock with a bull's eye lamp. He said it cost seven pence or eight pence.

We, all three, then went back to the Star and Garter. Orrock and I came out and we left Miles in there. We had a walk round, up towards the school to the chapel again. We went the same way as before and the prisoner said there were too many people about, he could not do the job then. He said he was going to get over the gates or else through a window that he had opened earlier when he'd spoken to the girl.

I then went to the Railway Tavern, where I saw Miles again. Orrock did not go with me, I left him by the chapel, under the wall next to the doorway where the window is. I don't know whether it is in Ashwin Street, or what street it was, but it was not far from the Railway Tavern, it was beside the little wall. At that time, he had the 1 1/4-inch chisel and the cold chisel, I kept the 7/8-inch one. I didn't see any wedge. He was dressed in a long black overcoat and light trousers and wore a wide-awake hat like this produced. I had it in my hand during the day and tried it on me and it fitted me. This is the one. I spoke to him about his appearance and said he looked like a parson. Before he left me, he said he would take the things he got from the chapel to his brother-in-law, Tilley, and he would melt them down.

After I had been with Miles in the Railway Tavern a little time, we heard something going off. I thought it was fog-signals, being a foggy night. I heard three shots. I then came out of the house and walked down the street and saw the policeman lying on his back opposite the gates of Paternoster's stables, there were some policemen there. Miles asked Sergeant Ash if he should fetch a doctor, but he did not go as they said they would take the poor fellow to the hospital. I then went home. Miles also went away, I left him near his home at the top of Wellington Road. I didn't know where he lived.

I saw nothing of the prisoner after the shots were fired. I didn't wait to see the constable taken to the hospital. Next morning, Saturday, I saw Miles. I next saw the prisoner when he came around, it must have been about three weeks afterwards I think, I can't exactly tell.'

In reply to a question by the Court, Evans responded, 'The prisoner did not want me to go along with him at first when this robbery was contemplated. I was to have a shilling or two next day if it came off all game, I was not to do anything.'

In response to Poland, Evans clarified, 'It was on a Saturday afternoon about three weeks afterwards when the prisoner came to me where I worked at Blade and Friar's, cabinetmakers, 12A, Hoxton Street. I was working there then. Young Pottinger was with him, he came around for some money I had for some tickets from his father, we had a benefit at the Cambridge. Before that, I had seen these bills about, but I never took any notice of them. I can read, but I never read them, I read a bit in the papers about it. I could not give him any money that Saturday. I asked him to treat me and took him to the Adam and Eve and he stood a pot of four ale there.

Evans went on. 'The first thing he said was, 'Are you going to put me away?' I said, 'No,' and he said, 'There are two hundred pounds for you if you do.' I said, 'No, I wouldn't for a thousand pounds.' I knew two hundred pounds had been offered, it was in the paper. The prisoner said Miles had taken an oath that if I informed he would put my light out and he asked me if I would do the same. I hesitated a little while and said I would. Nothing more was said.'

'I think we parted then,' Evans continued. 'The prisoner said he had just got married or was going to be married, I know he married shortly afterwards. Young Pottinger was present when this conversation took place, but I don't think he heard it. I next saw the prisoner on a tramcar sometime after, coming from Tottenham, we were both coming together to our work. He said, 'I went to see the policeman buried. If he hadn't struggled he would never have got shot.' He said he was along with some of the detectives on the tramcar and he had ridden on the tramcar many a time and had talked about the affair, but they never knew he was the one that did it.

'The prisoner told me that when the policeman had asked him what he was doing, he'd come out and thrown the revolver away. The policeman had tried to pick it up and there had been a struggle for it and the prisoner said that if he had not struggled he would never have got shot. He was going to go along quietly if the policeman hadn't picked up the pistol.'

'The prisoner showed me his trousers on the tram. I never took much notice of them. He said he had cut his trousers knee and cut his hand in the struggle. I did not take any notice of the trousers. He said they were the trousers he had on. He said after the struggle he went straight home. He asked me why I didn't pick up his hat. I said, 'How did I know you had dropped it? Or else I would have picked it up.' Nobody heard this conversation on the tramcar, the only man on it along with me was Edward Blade, the man I lodged with and he did not hear the conversation. The prisoner did not tell me what became of the revolver. He said he had got it from an advertisement in the paper.'

'I did not see the prisoner again till I saw him at Bow Street last month. Before that, I think on 29th July, Sergeant Cobb came to where I worked and Miles was with him. I afterwards made a statement to Mr Glass of what I knew about the matter. That was the first time I gave information against the prisoner and I would not have done so then if I had not been taken up. I, afterwards, made a further statement and was examined as a witness at Bow Street.'

Cross-examined by Mr Fulton, Evans stated, 'I had been on the drink for a week. I was not drunk on the night in question, nor was I suffering from the effects. I had got sober. Orrock and Miles did not want me to go with them. I did not know they had arranged to enter the chapel till we came from the Walford. I heard it then, they wanted me to leave them. I said, 'Go on, I will come along with you, I should have had a share in it, a couple of shillings perhaps.'

'Like a good many chaps would, I wanted to see what was going on. I should not have got any profit out of it. Miles and Orrock said, 'You will have a bob or two tomorrow if it comes off all right.' That was the reason I remained. I saw the pistol at the Walford first and last between 7pm and 8pm, I never saw it again. I do not know what became of it. I asked Orrock to let me look at it and I pointed it at him and he turned his head. I gave it back to him, I am quite sure of that. I did not see Miles with it at all on that night, I am quite sure of that.'

'Orrock said he had the pistol in case anybody should interfere with him in getting into the chapel. That was what I put it down to. After I heard what I thought were fog signals, we went out and saw the policeman lying on the ground. I did not know whether he was shot or not, I could not tell, I was not a doctor. I saw a pool of congealed blood that his head was in and I said it might have been Tom that did it. I did not make any statement at that time, I was not sure it was him.'

'I saw Miles next morning. I said to Miles that night, 'I reckon it was young Tom that done it.' I saw him on a Saturday morning by accident and I saw him again at the Hen and Chicken at Highbury a long time afterwards, just before they fetched me from my work. I had not seen him again until July this year. I read about the reward in the paper, not in the bill. I had seen the bill, I saw the bill posted up at police stations and other places a day or so after the policeman was shot. I never stop to read bills at police stations much. I did not see any bills except at one place at Stamford Hill, in a bootmaker's shop. I did not read it then, I only cast my eye on it as I went past.'

'I had no curiosity to know what the two hundred pounds referred to. I knew it referred to Cole because I read it in the Sunday paper. When I saw Orrock again, I said to him, 'God strike me dead, I will put his light out if he talks.' I was referring to Miles. I said that because Orrock said to me that Miles had taken an oath that he would put my light out if I informed. I was not to take any part in breaking into the chapel, I only drank the beer.'

Mr Fulton then asked the witness, 'Then you had nothing to be afraid of, there was no reason why you should not give information?'

'What, tell on my own pal, my shop-mate, I certainly would not tell on my own pal,' Evans replied. 'I only gave the statement I have spoken of when I saw Miles with the police. I did not know what Miles had said about the matter. I had been told he had given his statement and some other persons had been giving statements and they told me to speak the truth and I spoke the truth, I was bound to do so then.'

'I was told there had been a lot spoken about me, but I did not mind that. I did not hear it said that I and Miles were to keep watch outside the chapel, I never heard it. I should have given a whistle if anybody had come near, it was so dark you could see nothing before you. It was arranged that I was to give a whistle if it was wanted. Miles was going inside the chapel, so they said. Orrock started on the job first, I mean he put it up.

'I did not give any whistle on that night. I was not outside in Ashwin Street at a quarter-past 10, I was inside the Railway Tavern drinking beer. I did not give the whistle because he went to do the job too quickly. I was along with him as he passed the wall where he got over and then I went to the Railway Tavern and had a pint of four ale. I did not see him get over the wall, it was a low wall and he told me he got over afterwards. I left him when he was going to get over. He stood there a little while, he stood by where he got over, but I did not know he was going to get over so quick.'

'I went to the Railway Tavern. Miles was there. I swear that it was not arranged that a pistol was to be fired off as a signal if any policeman came up. I never had a pistol. I asked the prisoner what he wanted the revolver for. He said in case anybody interfered with him and I said, 'Good luck.' I meant if anybody interfered with him, 'Pop him off.' I thought that a proper thing to do under the circumstances.'

'Pottinger was with us in the Adam and Eve when the conversation took place that I have spoken of. He did not hear, he was a little way behind. Two can speak without a third one hearing, can't they? I was dressed in a light overcoat and a black-and-white scarf. It is in the shop now, I took it off before I came here this morning. I cannot say how Miles was dressed, I think he had a white choker on or a white scarf round his neck. I cannot say what clothes he had on, I don't think he had an overcoat on, I cannot tell, or what coloured trousers he had. He was wearing a hat something like mine, a hard, black hat. I cannot recollect whether he had a long dark overcoat on, I cannot tell what colour it was but he must have had a coat on.'

In reply to a re-examination by Mr Poland, Evans declared, 'I am quite sure that when I heard the first report, which I thought was a fog signal, I and Miles were inside the Railway Tavern. I swear it was not till we heard the third shot that we came out. We came out both together.

Frederick Miles was next to provide evidence and again the weight that would be given to the testimony warrants its inclusion in full:-

'I now live at 9, Eudell Street, Shacklewell, Stoke Newington. On Friday, 1 December 1882, I was living at 2, Wellington Road, Stoke Newington. I knew the prisoner at that time, I have known him somewhere about 10 years.

I met him that day by accident. I afterwards saw Evans. I met Mortimer at the corner of the turning where he lived. I and the prisoner and Evans were together part of that day and later, we went to the Star and Garter and afterwards to the Walford. We got there between 5:30 and 6 o'clock. I went home from there and had tea and came back afterwards.

We three were together at about 8 o'clock. The prisoner said he was going to the Baptist Chapel in Ashwin Street to fetch away some plate. He asked me if I was going anywhere particular. I said, 'No.' I told him I would go with him and he said, 'Very well.' He said he wanted me to help him to carry the plate away and he said he was going to take it to his brother-in-law's, Tilley. He said he used to pay for a seat at the chapel.

I saw some chisels. These are the two I saw, the 1 1/4-inch and the cold chisel. He had some more, but he gave Evans those. I did not see them. I saw these in his hand in the Walford when I came back from tea, he did not say anything about these chisels. I did not see any revolver that night or any wedge, nothing was said about a revolver in my presence. I knew he had a revolver before that night.

I, Orrock and Evans left the Walford together and went to the Railway Tavern. We stopped in there a little while and Orrock went out and came back again, at somewhere about 9 o'clock. He said there were too many people about, then he went out again. Evans went with him, then I went out. I did not join them then. I walked to the corner of Dalston Lane and I saw Orrock and Evans coming across the road opposite the lamp shop.

Evans said Orrock was going to buy a lamp. Orrock was then walking towards the lamp shop, he afterwards came back. I did not see the lamp and he did not say anything about it, he came back and joined us and we went and had some drink at the Railway Tavern. Orrock went out again, I did not see where he went and I did not see him again that night.

Evans went out for some time and came back and when we were there together I heard a report. We thought they were some fog signals going off. I heard two or three reports then we came out. I saw somebody running by the door and I looked down Ashwin Street and went down to opposite Paternoster's stables in Beech Street and there saw the policeman lying on the ground.

I saw blood there. I saw Sergeant Ash and asked him if I should fetch a doctor. I don't know where Evans was, I don't know whether he left the Railway Tavern with me. They did not want me to fetch a doctor, they said they would take the poor fellow to the hospital. I saw Evans afterwards, standing at the back of me, near where the constable was. I afterwards went away home and Evans too.

The prisoner was dressed that night in a long black coat, mixture trousers, and a soft felt hat. Evans put on the hat during the day, he took it from Orrock and tried it on and said it fitted him nicely. I say the hat produced is the one he wore that night. I never saw the prisoner again till I was at Bow Street.

In October, I'd met the prisoner and Mortimer in Stoke Newington Road and they told me they were going down to Tottenham to buy a revolver. The prisoner said it was advertised in the Exchange and Mart and he showed me the advertisement. I read it. I and Mortimer and the prisoner went together to Vicarage Road, the place mentioned in the advertisement.

The prisoner left us there, I saw him go about a dozen doors down Vicarage Road to a private house. He returned in a short time and said he had bought the revolver and that he had seen a young woman, the governor was not at home. He showed me the revolver. It was a small silver-plated one, smaller than this produced I think, a smaller handle than that I should think, otherwise it was the same as that. It was a pin-fire. There were also some small cartridges, twenty or thirty, with a pin sticking out of them. On our way back, it was suggested we should try the revolver and the prisoner fired at a tree. Mortimer was still with us, it was at some place between Vicarage Road and the railway bridge at the Lea, in Tottenham Marches.

I knew of this bill being issued, I never gave any information to the police until Sergeant Cobb came to me at the end of May this year. He spoke to me and I then made a statement to him. I told him about this matter, I should have done so before if it had not been for that bill. I did not want the two hundred pounds, I did not want people to think I wanted the two hundred pounds. I took Sergeant Cobb and pointed out the place where the shot had been fired at the tree and I saw him find the bullet.'

Under cross-examination from Mr Fulton, Miles stated, 'I was not anxious to give information, I would have given information but for the bill. I don't know when I first saw the bill, it is a long time ago, it might have been three or four days after 1st December, I don't exactly know the day. I first saw it at the police-station as I was going by.'

'I did not make any statement when I came up and saw the policeman on the ground, because I did not know anything about it then, I did not know who had done it then. It never occurred to me how he had got on the ground, I heard he had been shot but I did not know who had done it. It first occurred to me when I was going home. Evans said he should not be at all surprised if it was not Orrock, but I did not know that it was the truth. I had not seen the prisoner, I did not know it was right, I had not seen him after the policeman was shot, I had seen him a few moments before.'

'Sergeant Cobb first came to me a long time afterwards and then I did not believe a word of it. I did not say before the Magistrate, 'He mentioned one word and then I knew what he came about.' He asked me if I knew the prisoner, Orrock. I had not before that heard rumours that statements had been made about what I had been doing that night. I have no idea how Sergeant Cobb came to me. When he asked me if I knew Orrock, of course, I said I did. He asked me what I knew and I told him and it was produced into writing.'

'I was not anxious to get rid of Evans on this night of 1st December, nor was Orrock that I know of. He was more a companion of Orrock's than mine because I had never seen him before, at least I'd never been in his company before. I and Orrock had not arranged together to share the results of this entry into the chapel. I knew he was going to attempt to enter the chapel, but he did not say he was going to commit a robbery there. He said he was going to fetch some plate. I did not understand what that meant, I never asked him any questions. I never asked him what he was going to do. I did not understand he was going to steal the plate. I knew he belonged to the chapel, I did not know he was going to get the plate. I had been out all day enjoying myself I did not ask him anything about that.'

'Orrock came back into the Railway Tavern and said there were too many people about, but he did not say it distinctly to me. I overheard him saying it. I did not speak to him. I did not know what he meant then. It is not true I was to help him to dispose of the plate to his brother-in-law, we did not make any arrangement to do it. It was to be taken to his brother-in-law's.'

'I did not say anything about melting the plate down, I did not know whether it was to be melted down, or what he was going to do with it. He said he was going to take it to his brother-in-law's. I may have said before the Magistrate that he told me it was to be taken to his brother-in-law's to be melted down, I did not know what for. I was to have a share in the matter, he was going to give me something. I don't know what, for helping him to carry it away.'

'It was not arranged that Evans was to be outside and give a whistle if any policeman came up, nothing of the kind. I was not to do anything of that sort. I had not the revolver in my hand at all that night, I will swear I had not. I did not see Evans with it, I never saw it that night and nothing was said about it in my presence.

'I had on a hard, felt hat that night and, I think, a white scarf, no overcoat. I had on a short pilot coat. Evans had on an overcoat, a long one. I don't know the colour. I think it was a brown coat. It was a foggy night, rather thick. I saw Orrock go out of the Railway Tavern the last time and neither I nor Evans followed him the last time. Evans went out for a short time after that by himself and he came back as the fog-signals, as I thought, were going off. I went out once before that, I went to the corner. I did not go out at all between the time Orrock went out and hearing the fog-signals.'

'I have known the prisoner a great many years. I don't know about his giving me an overcoat at any time, I used to have a lot of clothes from him at one time. He had not given me an overcoat about 1st December, not of any kind. I was going to be a conductor of a tramcar about that time. He did not, shortly before 1st December, give me a long overcoat for my being a conductor of a tramcar. I am quite sure about that.'

The third of the witness statements included in full is that of Police Sergeant Frederick Cobb:-

'On Friday night, 1st December 1882, I was passing through Abbott Street, down Beech Street, at about a quarter-past nine with a constable named Brockwell. I noticed a man alone, standing about three or four yards from a lamp-post. He was looking towards the Baptist Chapel door and I saw his face. I was coming off duty. I spoke to Brockwell, then I went past the chapel to the police-station and then I went home to bed from the police-station.

After I had been in bed, at a quarter-past eleven Brockwell came to me and in consequence of what he said I got up and subsequently, I gave a description of the man I had seen standing by the lamp on Beech Street. It was from that description the handbills were published.

This is a handbill (Cobb identified the item produced in Court). This description is correct. (The bill was entered as evidence and read in part to the Court. It gave a description of the murderer as, age twenty-one, height five-foot-two, complexion pale, round face, slight moustache, dressed in a long dark overcoat and light trousers). I gave a description of the hat as being a black soft felt hat.

On 1st February 1884, I went to Coldbath Fields Prison. I went in with a warder and there were about seven men there in one of the large waiting-rooms of the prison. I went there to see if I could identify the man I had seen on the night of 1st December 1882. I first picked out a man on the left of the prisoner, he looked very much like him, but as the men were filing out of the room I caught the prisoner's side face and at once told Inspector Glass. I had not seen his side face before. The prisoner could not hear what I said. The men were all taken out and brought back again and placed in a different position and I then picked the prisoner out. I have since had opportunities of seeing him and I am positive he is the man I saw on that night.

The day after 1st December 1882, I went with another police constable to Ashwin Street and there found, under the stonework of the doorway of house number three, about six feet from the top stone step, a mark on a brick. It looked like a bullet mark. I found a similar mark by the gutter pipe between houses numbers three and five. Underneath the place on house number three where I saw the bullet mark, there was some brick-dust, as if just cut away. I am accustomed to pistol shots and in my opinion, a pistol shot would make a mark like that.

In consequence of a statement made by two men, Frederick Miles and Henry Mortimer, I went, on 28th July 1884, with Miles to Tottenham Marshes and he pointed out a tree to me with a small wooden post in front of it. The spot where the tree is lies halfway between the Ferry Boat public-house and the railway bridge over the Lea. In consequence of a statement made by Miles to me, I examined the tree and from it, about four feet from the ground, I cut out this bullet with a chisel (the bullet was in a packet and marked as evidence). I went the same day, in consequence of what Miles said to me, to a place called Vicarage Road to endeavour to find the place where the pistol was bought, but I failed to do so. Numbers twenty-one and twenty-three were empty houses.'

Under cross-examination from Fulton, Cobb clarified, 'I was in bed at the time Cole met with his death. It was a quarter-past nine when I saw this man on Beech Street. The description of the man is correct that I saw on Beech Street at a quarter-past nine.'

When re-examined by Mr Poland, Cobb revised his statement regarding his visit to Vicarage Road. He corrected himself and stated that number twenty-three had been an empty house and he had gone to number twenty-one, which had been occupied, but the couple that had sold the pistol no longer resided there.

By the end of the first day, all the witnesses for the prosecution were heard and the case for the prosecution was concluded. The trial was adjourned and the jury was taken to a hotel for the night.

The next day began with a summing-up of the case for the Crown, presented by Mr Poland, who clarified that it was not for the prisoner to prove his innocence, but for the prosecution to prove his guilt beyond all reasonable doubt. Had the evidence adduced before the jury on the part of the Crown done this? Poland asserted that the story told by the witnesses had, unquestionably, been a remarkable one.

Referring to the evidence of Miles, Evans and the other acquaintances of Orrock that had been called, Poland observed that he could not ask the jury to return a guilty verdict on the sole and uncorroborated evidence of those persons, but asked that they remember the witnesses were the prisoner's friends. He put it to the jury that while Orrock may be considered to have been unfortunate in the selection of his acquaintances, this was not the fault of the prosecution.

Poland asked that the jury recollect that only one man was seen in the street during the struggle with the policeman and that man had left his hat behind. The prisoner had been a seat-holder in the chapel and was fully aware of the sacramental plate he had planned to steal.

The prosecutor turned his attention again to the prisoner's companions, noting that if the evidence of men of their character stood by itself then he believed it would be the duty of the jury to view it with caution. He asked the jury to note, however, that the testimony they had provided was backed up by important particulars, meaning their statements could not be set aside as mere invention. They had identified the hat and chisel found by the police as having belonged to the prisoner. Other important points in the evidence of Miles and Evans had, Poland claimed, been fully corroborated by other independent witnesses.

Poland warned the jury that the defence would attack the evidence provided by Miles and Evans and would likely contend that although he might have intended to commit the burglary, the prisoner was not the person who had shot the constable. Poland argued that on every important point in the case, there was ample corroboration of the story the two men had told.

There was no doubt the three men had been together on the night in question and Poland asked the jury if they could possibly believe Miles and Evans would have come forward at this point, having not taken the opportunity of earning the reward on offer, just to concoct a story about the prisoner. He offered that when the jury came to consider the matter fully, he would submit to their good judgment and common sense that the case had been fully proved against the prisoner at the bar.

In conclusion, the prosecutor stated that the policemen of the great metropolis of London had arduous, difficult and dangerous duties to perform and from time to time, unarmed as they were, they had to arrest and detain criminals who were armed. On such occasions, the public, whose servants they were and for whose protection they were employed, expected them, with courage and determination, to do their duty.

On this occasion, Poland continued, no one could doubt that police officer George Cole had acted with courage and determination. Where a constable was killed outright in the execution of his duty and there may be no eyewitnesses to the act, it would be deplorable indeed, Poland offered, that if the crime could be proved by other evidence, the criminal should escape. If, after a full and careful investigation, the facts proved before the jury satisfied them beyond all reasonable doubt of the guilt of the accused, it was their bounden duty, by the oaths they had taken, to return a verdict according to the evidence.

Mr Fulton then rose to his feet to address the jury on behalf of the prisoner.

Fulton informed the jury that he recognised there could be no graver responsibility someone could be brought face to face with than that of having to determine whether another person was guilty of the crime of wilful murder. He then said he had no doubt there were other cases of murder in which a jury could convict someone of the lesser crime of manslaughter, but he was bound to say that it seemed to him, because the law had always thrown a protective arm around police officers in the execution of their duty, no such alternative option was available to this jury.

If a policeman met his death in the execution of his duty, Fulton went on, the person who killed him was, by the law, guilty of murder. It, therefore, became very necessary for the jury to consider, with the greatest care, the circumstances of the case and to ask themselves whether, so far as the prisoner was concerned, the case had been made out to their satisfaction.

Moving on, Fulton told the jury he thought what had been proved was that, young as he was, Orrock had made some very evil companions, amongst whom were the witnesses Miles and Evans. He put it to the jury that despite his denial, Miles was, whether by arrangement made or not, planning to participate in the attempt to enter the chapel to get possession of the sacramental plate and take it to the prisoner's brother-in-law to be melted.

The defence lawyer asked the jury to compare the brutal frankness of Evan's testimony with the evasiveness of the testimony provided by Miles. Evans had not tried to disguise the fact he was fully aware of the planned robbery and was to participate, to some extent, in the proceeds if successful. Evans had also made it clear Orrock and Miles had tried to get rid of him, but he had refused to leave. That the men had intended to get into the chapel had, Fulton offered, been proved. There was, therefore, ample corroboration of the charge of attempting to break into the chapel, but that should not be taken as corroboration of the charge of murder against the prisoner.

Fulton contested that it was quite likely an older offender, one who had been convicted many times, reckless of life and fearing that at any time the police might lay hands on him, might go about armed to resist apprehension. It was less likely a youth of twenty-one would be armed for such a purpose and it was an essential element of the case that Orrock was armed for that specific purpose. Although there may have been evidence the prisoner was possessed of a revolver, it was, Fulton opined, highly improbable he would use it on the police.

The barrister then asked the jury to consider the atmospheric conditions which existed on the night in question. It had been a foggy day, but the mist was beginning to clear by 10pm and it would have been hazardous for a man to try to break into a chapel, on a thoroughfare like Ashwin Street, at such an early hour in the night, without having a confederate on the outside to give him a signal on the approach of police or anyone likely to intrude.

Fulton argued that Miles and Evans had agreed to assist the prisoner and the pistol was to be fired, by one or the other, as a signal to Orrock of the approach of the police, the fog preventing any other form of signal being given. The only evidence the revolver was not in the possession of Miles or Evans on that night rested solely upon their own statements. The evidence provided by the two men, Fulton ventured, was such that the jury would require the fullest corroboration before acting upon it. He declared that it was not incumbent upon him to prove who fired the fatal shot, but that all he was required to do was to show, by sufficient arguments upon the evidence, that there was no proof at all the prisoner had fired the shot.

Turning his attention to the evidence of identification,

Fulton pointed out that the three men were of a similar size and the description of the man struggling with the policeman might easily have applied, with equal force, to any of the three.

The evidence of Orrock's sister had revealed the prisoner had returned home having lost his hat and torn the knee of his trousers. That evidence would only have been important, Fulton contested, if the prisoner was being tried upon the charge of burglary and he was not disputing the prisoner had attempted to break into the chapel. This acceptance of being at the scene to commit a burglary also rendered the identification of Orrock by Sergeant Cobb as being irrelevant.

Returning to Miles, Fulton said he believed the man had gone out of his way to ingratiate himself with the jury when he had claimed he would have given information beforehand had it not been for the fact he had not wished to be thought to be taking blood money, due to the reward on offer. This did not hold up to scrutiny, as the handbills had not been issued until 4 December and if they had known who fired the shot, Miles and Evans had the opportunity to go directly to the police-station before the reward was offered. Fulton pointed out discrepancies in the evidence of the two men and ventured that having been concerned with the prisoner in attempting to break into the chapel, they had bound themselves with a most solemn obligation to remain silent.

Switching his attention to the idea one of the witnesses may have been the shooter, Fulton suggested Miles was just the kind of man to use a revolver if a policeman was to lay hands upon him. He then asked the jury to recall the brutal frankness of Evan's testimony in the witness box and told them it was his belief the man had considered it to be a praiseworthy and meritorious thing to shoot a police constable. Fulton put to the jury that Miles and Evans had become aware rumours were afloat about them having been involved with Orrock in the attempt to break into the chapel and the men had found it necessary to protect themselves. He claimed there was insufficient evidence to justify the jury reaching the conclusion it had been Orrock who had fired the shots that had killed the policeman.

In conclusion, Fulton stated that although a young man in the prime of life and in the gallant and faithful discharge of his duty had met his death at the hands of an assailant, the jury should not forget there was another young man, standing upon the very threshold of his life, to whom the matter was of the most vital importance. He told the jury he was sure they would give the case their most anxious and careful consideration and said he trusted they would be guided to a righteous and just conclusion to the matter.

It was now left for Mr Justice Hawkins to sum up the entire case for the jury. He began by observing that the jury had been addressed with very great ability by counsel on both sides. The Judge then advised it was now for the jury to calmly and carefully look at all the evidence and to ask themselves, solemnly, what conclusion they came to upon it.

If the case was not established, the prisoner was, as a matter of right, entitled to be acquitted. On the other hand, the Judge continued, if the evidence, after being sifted by them, led them irresistibly to the conclusion the prisoner's was the hand that shot the poor young man in the discharge of his duty, the jury must faithfully discharge the painful duty cast upon them and according to their oaths and consciences, return that verdict which they thought ought to be returned.

The case was one of vital importance, Hawkins declared,

not only to the prisoner but to the public at large, for if the young man Cole had been murdered and slaughtered in the execution of his duty by the prisoner, it was right and fit that the law should avenge that terrible outrage.

The Judge then asked the jury to consider, not whether it was possible to raise any fanciful or imaginary doubt in the matter, but whether the case was brought home to their minds with that amount of certainty which they would require before they would act in any important event in their lives. The law was, that if a constable in the execution of his duty found a man in the act of committing a felony, which burglary and sacrilege most unquestionably was, he was justified in arresting him on the spot. If in trying to evade and prevent his arrest, the person used a deadly weapon against the man who had him in custody and used it in such a manner as to cause the man's death, he would be liable for the crime of wilful murder.

It was the opinion of the Judge that Mr Fulton had done no injustice or harm to his client in frankly admitting to the jury that he could see no alternatives, on the present occasion, but murder or acquittal. The learned counsel had not asked the jury to reduce the crime to one of manslaughter because, having regard to the state of the law, he could not do so.

Hawkins told the jury they had to ask themselves whether there was any doubt the gallant young officer who was on duty on the night in question did arrest some person who was engaged in the felonious act of breaking into the Baptist Chapel. He was sure the jury would have, long ago, made up their minds on that subject and he did not think Mr Fulton had contended the officer was exceeding his duty or was not faithfully and courageously performing it.

The Judge was of the view that Mr Fulton had not attempted to deny the person the constable was struggling with was the one who had shot him, adding that there was not a particle of evidence to suggest otherwise. The real question was whether the prisoner had committed the act. That depended not merely upon the testimony of the several witnesses whose evidence had been so adversely commented upon by the counsel for the defence, but on other testimony on which he thought no such observations could be made.

Hawkins then reviewed, at length, the evidence given during the trial and discussed the important question of corroboration regarding the evidence of Miles and Evans, whose statements, he suggested, made on different occasions, differed slightly. It had been stated in the evidence that Miles and Evans, who had been drinking together in a public-house, went to the scene of the shooting when they heard the shots fired and Miles had asked a policeman whether he should try and fetch a doctor. It would be for the jury to decide whether the two men would have run towards the crime scene to assist, as all the evidence had suggested, if they had been directly involved in the shooting.

The Judge offered that the jury could not have listened to the very able address of Mr Fulton without feeling it had been, indirectly, suggested that Evans was the murderer. If one was to suppose Evans was to be placed on trial for the offence, Hawkins asked, what particle of evidence would enable the jury to even entertain a suspicion of his guilt? Evans had not been shown to have a revolver, the chisels were not his, he did not lose his hat or tear his clothes and he had not been seen to be involved in a struggle with anyone. There was, therefore, no tangible proof to implicate Evans and the Judge informed the jury he believed it right to point this out.

Finally, Hawkins reiterated that it was for the jury to consider all the facts and to give their verdict based upon them. If they were to conclude the case had not been made out to their satisfaction, the prisoner was entitled to an acquittal. If, however, when they came to review all the circumstances, they should think the chain of evidence was too strong for them to take that view, they should find him guilty.

The jury retired to consider their verdict at 1:20pm and had finished their considerations by 1:40pm, finding Thomas Orrock guilty of wilful murder.

Asked by the Judge whether he had anything to say as to why a sentence of death should not be passed upon him, Orrock replied firmly, 'I have no more to say, my lord, than that I am not guilty.'

Justice Hawkins donned his black cap before pronouncing, 'Thomas Henry Orrock, notwithstanding your asseveration to the contrary, I am satisfied the jury has come to an honest, righteous and just conclusion in finding you guilty of the crime of wilful murder. I think it was impossible for any human being to listen to the evidence given against you and come to any other conclusion than that it was absolutely clear to demonstration it was you who took the life of that brave young officer while he was discharging his duty to the public.'

Hawkins continued. 'There is no single circumstance in the case in your favour. I have thought it over for hours, carefully and anxiously, with a view to seeing whether there was an escape for you from the doom which awaits you. I am sorry to say, every single circumstance in the case does, more and more, satisfy me that the evidence against you was irresistible and that you now stand, justly and righteously, convicted of wilful murder. You slew, while he was in the discharge of his duty, that brave young officer and cut short his days by your murderous hand. For that crime, the law says you must die.'

A solemn sermon followed. 'I do entreat you to remember that, henceforth, this world is no more for you and I hope, when you descend the steps from the dock where you now stand, you will turn your heart and your thoughts to Almighty God and pray for forgiveness for your great sin. It now only remains for me to pass upon you the sentence of the law.'

An unmoved Orrock stared blankly forward as the Judge passed a sentence of death upon him. After Orrock had been removed, Hawkins told the jury they had made a presentment with which he cordially agreed.

The jury had stated that they wished to express their unqualified approval of the way Inspector Glass had investigated the murder of Police-Constable Cole. The Judge declared he was in complete agreement and thought it right to add that Sergeant Cobb and the other officers who had taken part in the case deserved a great deal of approval from the public at large for having, very carefully, investigated this very important case to ensure justice had been done.

With that, the Court rose and a very satisfied group of policemen returned to the streets, content in the knowledge that the man who had killed their late colleague had been brought to justice.

Thomas Orrock was hanged at Newgate on 6 October 1884.

For Scotland Yard, the case provided a perfect example of the lengths to which police officers would go to track down the killer of one of their own. Sergeant Cobb, in particular, had never lost sight of the case and had doggedly pursued every possible lead during the almost twenty-one-month period that elapsed between the shooting of Constable Cole and the first appearance in the Police Court of Thomas Orrock.

This investigation is widely considered to be the first example of the Metropolitan Police using ballistics evidence in a case. The recovery of the bullets Orrock had fired into the tree in Tottenham Marches during his target practice was inspired and their match with the bullets recovered at the scene was vital in corroborating the evidence provided by Orrock's rather unsavoury 'friends'.

Constable Cole was buried in Abney Park Cemetery. His wife, who died in 1911, was later buried in the same grave. It is a testimony to the undying respect the Metropolitan Police have for their fallen colleagues that, following the re-discovery and restoration of the grave a full one hundred and thirty years after the death of Police-Constable George Cole, a memorial service was held at Abney Park Cemetery, on 30 November 2012, to pay tribute to the policeman. The event was attended by Hackney police officers, members of the local community, the local councillor and the minister of the local church. Hackney's Borough Police Commander laid a wreath and addressed the gathering before a two-minute silence was observed in memory of George Cole and other fallen officers.

4 ANARCHY IN THE UK

Following the relative failure of the Russian Revolution of 1905, a revolution driven by mass strikes, peasant revolt and military mutiny, a new approach to forcing change emerged, political terrorism. The rise of the Russian Anarchist movement heralded a period when assassination would become the preferred choice for bringing about radical change.

A backlash was inevitable. The number of punitive death sentences grew rapidly and the wide-scale incarceration of political prisoners became commonplace. The displaced and the disgruntled began to spread into Western Europe. London quickly became a favoured destination for these political refugees. Upon arrival in Great Britain, immigrants were free to travel within the country without restriction, a freedom of movement not afforded throughout the rest of Europe. Great Britain also placed heavy restrictions on the police with regards to the interrogation of new arrivals from the Continent.

The Autonomie Club, based in Windmill Street, Tottenham Court Road, was originally founded by Germans in the late eighteen-eighties, but soon became a central meeting-place for 'international' anarchists from France, Italy, Spain, Holland and Belgium. The club was believed to have had up to seven hundred members at one time and preached of change through violence and assassination via its official publication 'Die Autonomie', which was widely circulated throughout Europe.

145

Other extremist groups then began to set up around London. The Russian Nihilists in the East End, the Armenian Revolutionists in Shepherd's Bush and the Lettish Revolutionists in Leytonstone and Tottenham. The accepted method for raising funds to support these organisations was, 'by any means necessary'.

On 23 January 1909, seventeen-year-old Albert Keyworth was preparing for his weekly Saturday bank-run to the London and South-Western Bank in Hackney, to collect the wages for the employees of the rubber works owned by Mr Julius Schnurmann.

Keyworth was conveyed to the bank in the company car by Schnurmann's driver, Joseph Wilson. After a trouble-free trip, the two men returned to the factory, in Chestnut Road, with the wages safely in hand. The car drew neatly into the kerb. Keyworth opened the car door and was exiting the vehicle when, from the corner of his eye, he spotted two men standing, like the world's scruffiest sentries, on either side of the factory gate. On the right-hand side stood a dark-haired man Keyworth did not recognise and on the left, a fair-haired man whom he knew only as Jacob.

Believing the two men to be employees at the factory, Keyworth was not particularly concerned by their presence at the gate. He would have had every right to be concerned though. As he approached the gate, Keyworth was grabbed roughly from behind by Jacob, who tried to tear the money-bag from his grasp. The contents, paper bags containing gold, silver and copper amounting to eighty pounds, spilt to the ground. Keyworth frantically cried out for assistance from the driver, before he felt the silencing hand of his assailant close around his throat.

Joseph Wilson wasted no time in rushing to the aid of his beleaguered colleague. Jacob was on top of Keyworth, who was valiantly struggling to free himself. Wilson threw himself at the assailant, knocking him off the boy but in the process of doing so tumbling to the ground himself. It was only then that he looked up to see the cold-eyed, dark-haired man pointing a revolver straight at him. Time froze momentarily before the sound of the gun discharging brought the reality of the situation sharply back into focus.

Gas-stoker George Smith was casually making his way to work when he was startled by the sound of a gun-shot and desperate cries for help. With scant regard for his own safety, Smith bravely rushed towards the chaotic scene. By this time, each of the assailants was brandishing a revolver. Smith rugby-tackled one of the men, but as he lay helpless on the ground, he was shot at several times by the other gunman.

Smith soon saw he had taken a bullet to the chest. Fortunately, the gas stokers heavy works-clothing had cushioned the blow and the damage was not as bad as he first feared. Incredibly, after receiving treatment at the scene from a doctor, George Smith would soon be back on his feet and heading off to begin his shift. Quite a man.

The master criminals, who would later be identified as Paul Hefeld and Jacob Lepidus, did not seem to have taken account of the fact Chestnut Road Police Station was located directly across from the factory. On hearing the commotion at the shooting scene from within the Police Station, Police-Constables Albert Newman and William Tyler rushed to assist and saw the two armed assailants standing over George Smith. Spooked by the sight of the two fast-approaching policemen, Hefeld and Lepidus took flight, letting loose a volley of wild shots as they ran off down Chestnut Grove. As the policemen took up the chase and pursued the gunmen into Scales Road, a car pulled alongside them.

The car slowed, allowing Newman to jump inside while Tyler, who in his haste to assist had not had time to put on his police helmet, ran alongside the vehicle. Inside the vehicle was the company driver, Joseph Wilson, who informed Newman of his belief that the gunmen may have already emptied their revolvers. Newman prompted Wilson to attempt to run the two fleeing men down. As the chase proceeded into Mitchley Road, the car began to close in on Hefeld and Lepidus.

Wilson was to be proved wrong in his assertion that the men had run out of ammunition, as they quickly turned and fired at the vehicle. A bullet was sent through the front windscreen and out through the back window. A second bullet grazed Newman's cheek and a further bullet struck the car radiator, releasing a fountain of water and bringing the vehicle to a shuddering halt.

Albert Keyworth, having taken up the chase on foot from the factory gates, arrived on the scene to be greeted by the sight of the stricken car and of a child lying nearby. Blood was gushing from the child's mouth in a cruel mirror-image of the water gushing from the car radiator.

Ralph Joscelyne, a ten-year-old boy who had simply been ambling down the road, had tried to take cover behind the car and had been struck by a stray bullet. The boy had staggered across the road before crashing to the ground by the edge of the pavement. Mrs Elizabeth Andrews, who'd been alerted to the chase by the sound of police whistles and gunfire, saw the prone body of the boy and ran to his aid.

Mrs Andrews carefully lifted the limp body of the boy and carried him towards the car. When she realised the car was out of commission, the trembling woman stopped a passing cyclist, William Dormer, and urged him to take the child to the local hospital. As Dormer frantically made his way towards the hospital, cradling the boy in his arms, he could only look on in horror as he saw the life drain from the body of the pitiful child.

Keyworth silently surveyed the carnage as the chase continued into Park View Road.

As the pursuit passed a giant dust-destructor, an old-style waste incineration plant, the super-fit Tyler began to close in on the fleeing men. With the two men cornered, Tyler shouted, 'Come on, give in, the game is up!' Hefeld then turned and took deliberate aim, before putting a bullet into the head of the unarmed policeman.

Joseph Wilson, who had re-joined the chase on foot after abandoning the car, found himself having to dive behind the wall of the dust-destructor as his arrival was met with a fresh volley of gunfire. Wilson followed as Hefeld and Lepidus crossed a railway line then waded across Pymme's Brook. The men raced along the bank of the River Lea before crossing at Chalk Bridge, where they made a brief stand and resumed firing. The two fleeing men then cut through a field leading past the local reservoirs on the Tottenham Marshes and took refuge behind some hay-stacks.

By this stage, the chasing group had been joined by Police-Constable Bond. Bond borrowed a pistol from one of his fellow pursuers but found himself out of range as he fired off four shots.

Police-Constable Newman spotted a group of men in the neighbouring fields who were out duck-shooting and shouted for them to fire at the two fugitives. The duck-shooters, initially startled by the drama unfolding before them, did not immediately open fire, but once they had taken in what was happening they too joined the chase.

Hefeld and Lepidus began to realise the chasing pack was now quite heavily armed. Taking the view that hay-stacks don't provide the best protection from bullets, they set off again. The two desperate men vaulted over fences and hedges, intermittently stopping to exchange gunfire with the ever-expanding hunting party.

The pursuing crowd, who seemed unperturbed by the regular gunfire coming their way, now included many armed and unarmed policemen together with people on foot, in cars, on bicycles and on horseback. Just when it seemed impossible for the situation to get any further out of control, the two fleeing men came upon a Leyton-bound tram-car in Chingford Road and jumped aboard.

The terrified driver had a revolver pressed to his head and was ordered to drive for dear life as shots were fired at the panicking passengers as they leapt like lemmings from the hijacked vehicle. The pursuing policemen commandeered another tram-car and it joined the increasingly frantic pursuit.

This mode of transport was utilised until Hefeld and Lepidus were informed by the tram-driver that they were approaching a police station. The two men jumped from the tram and fired a volley of shots at a passing horse-drawn milk cart. The cart-driver quickly scarpered and the men used the abandoned milk-cart to travel down Forest Road.

At the bottom of Forest Road, they spotted what they must have presumed to be a faster horse-drawn cart. The cart-driver was met with the now customary volley of gunfire and ran for cover. Hefeld and Lepidus took control of the cart and with one driving and the other standing firing randomly into the chasing crowd, they carried on with their escape attempt.

The group that had jumped on board the chasing tram had since disembarked and had stopped a private motor car. They set off in pursuit of the horse and cart and soon managed to overtake it, driving the car in front of the terrified horse and forcing the cart to come to a shuddering halt. This group were then met by a volley of wild shots as Hefeld and Lepidus leapt from the cart and ran off towards Chingford.

Fast reaching a state of exhaustion, the pursued men were horrified to find their way blocked by a high fence. Lepidus managed to summon up his last ounce of strength to scale the fence, but Hefeld stumbled and fell. As he lay helpless, watching his pursuers closing in, Hefeld made one last effort to escape justice. He pressed his revolver to his head and shot himself in the right temple.

This attempt to escape, like all his others, was doomed to fail. The bullet exited through the top of his head but did not provide the fatal wound that Hefeld craved. The captured man, drenched in blood, had his wounds bound by bandages crudely fashioned from his own clothing. He was immediately conveyed to The Prince of Wales Hospital in Tottenham. His only words at the time were, 'I feel cold.'

Lepidus, meantime, was still being hunted and his indiscriminate shooting continued as he crossed another railway line and ran behind the hedges leading into Hale End, Chingford. There he took refuge within 'Oak Cottage'.

The chasing pack arrived seconds later and were greeted by the sight of a terrified woman, Mrs Rolstone, the occupier of the cottage, rushing from the house carrying a child. The woman was closely followed by her husband Charles and the other children, all of whom were quickly led to safety by the police.

Lepidus had entered the property through the woodshed and had then made his way into the sitting room. He examined the hearth and stove and considered trying to hide in the chimney, but, thinking better of it, he instead made his way through the kitchen then up the winding stairs leading to the front bedroom.

As a piercing voice from the crowd hailed the appearance of a face at the bedroom window, shotgun and revolver shots were fired, shattering the upper sash of the window and peppering the bedroom ceiling. This was a time in England when the possession of private firearms was not prohibited and many individuals had retained weapons after serving, at home and abroad, in the armed services.

Police-Constable Charles Eagles appropriated a gun and a ladder and climbed up to peer into the bedroom window. He was greeted by the sight of a man pointing a gun towards him. Eagles tried to get off a shot from his own gun but it failed him. Eagles swiftly retreated, then, borrowing another of the many revolvers that had appeared on the scene, he entered the cottage. Police-Constables John Cater and Charles Dixon were already inside the cottage with Inspector Gould.

After gathering their thoughts, the four policemen charged up the stairs towards the bedroom. Eagles and Cater fired through the door, which sprung open to reveal Lepidus pointing his own gun towards the entrance. The policemen fired further shots and Lepidus, rather than exchanging gunfire, turned his revolver on himself and let loose his final bullet.

When the body was later examined by police divisional surgeon Dr Alcock, it was confirmed that Lepidus had died by his own hand. The body was removed from the scene and taken to the mortuary at Queen's Road, Walthamstow.

The official list of the deaths and injuries resulting from the chase gives some indication of the absolute mayhem that had ensued:-

Killed

Jacob Lepidus- found dead inside 'Oak Cottage'

Police-Constable Tyler- died, after admission to Tottenham Hospital, from a bullet wound in the head.

Ralph Joscelyne- aged 10, died from bullet wounds

Injured

Paul Hefeld- in a critical condition with a bullet wound in the head

Sidney Slater- horse dealer, shot in the left thigh

Police-Constable Newman- wounded in the face and twice shot in the right leg

Police-Constable Nichol- shot in the back and left leg

Cyril Burgess- aged 16, shot in the right ankle

William Darning- aged 13, shot in the leg

Arthur Wilmot- aged 15, bullet wound in the leg

George Harwood- aged 26, bullet wounds on two fingers

Mr Smith- shot in the neck (grazed)

Joseph Dayler- shot in the leg

William Thomas- aged 23, bullet wound in the elbow

Frederick Mortimer- aged 38, bullet wound in the chest and shoulder

George Conyard- aged 19, bullet wound in the chest

Edward Loveday- aged 63, shot through the neck

William Roker- shot in both legs

Details were later released regarding the deceased police officer.

Police-Constable Tyler had earned distinction as an athlete and his ability as a runner had, sadly, been a contributing factor in his murder. He had managed to out-distance the other pursuers by a considerable margin when he had been brought down.

Before joining the police force, Tyler had spent ten years in the Royal Garrison Artillery and had remained an Army Reserve. He had joined the Metropolitan Police Force in 1903 and had been stationed in Tottenham since 1906.

Superintendent Jenkins described Tyler as a conscientious police officer who had been previously commended for his services by the Justices, Judges and Grand Jury at the Middlesex Sessions. Jenkins stated that he had been so impressed by Tyler that, despite him having served for only a fairly short time in the force, he had intended to recommend the constable to the Police Commissioner for promotion within the next couple of months.

Neither of the criminals had yet been formally identified. Both were rumoured to be members of a gang of Russian Anarchists and the Special Services Department of Scotland Yard were called in to investigate.

Hefeld had spoken from his hospital bed but had refused to reveal his name. He said he was a native of Riga and had arrived in England about two years earlier. He was put under strict suicide watch.

A leading member of the Russian Revolutionary

Movement claimed the two men were members of the Lettish League, an organisation that advocated political terrorism. It was not thought there was any great political motivation for this crime though, a straightforward attempted robbery being assumed to be more likely. The revolutionist believed Hefeld and Lepidus were, almost certainly, criminals before they joined the revolutionary party. Their crime bore a strong resemblance to crimes being perpetrated on an almost daily basis around Russia.

During the official Inquest into the death of Jacob Lepidus, the body was formally identified by a Russian named Stanislaus Kolenski. Lepidus had lodged with Kolenski between December 1907 and March 1908.

The Coroner confirmed Lepidus had been killed by a bullet in the head that matched the bullets found in his own gun.

Unprompted, the Coroner then decided to provide his own 'State of the Nation' address. He offered that England had always opened her doors to all aliens, regardless of whether they had committed political crimes in their own country or not. Such people had a haven in England and provided they behaved themselves they could settle. He suggested that, if they then descended to robbery and murder, the time may come when they may find themselves returned to their own countries and left to the mercies of those who knew them best. Whilst it was proper for the authorities to have pity on others, the Coroner continued, he believed they had a responsibility, first and foremost, to show pity towards their own people.

The Inquest delivered a verdict of *felo de se*, literally 'felon of himself'. They commended Police-Constables Tyler,

Eagles and Newman, Detective Dixon and those of the public that assisted them. They then asked the Coroner to draw the attention of the Home Secretary to the dangers they believed the country now faced under the existing Aliens Act.

The Chief Magistrate, Sir Albert De Rutzen, set up a public appeal on behalf of the widow of Police-Constable Tyler. The widow would only have been entitled to a maximum compensation of £15 per annum from the police authorities. Mrs Tyler, who had recently been hospitalised and was in poor health, would be entirely dependent on what the police could allow her and on funds that would, hopefully, be raised by the appeal.

As of 26 January 1909, Paul Hefeld's condition was being described by his doctors as satisfactory and he was still under guard in the Prince of Wales General Hospital.

Rumours and scare stories were rife and one rumour had sprouted wings. Fear had spread of a possible assault on the hospital by an anarchist group and there were also fears the group intended to plant a bomb somewhere in the area.

At around 10am on 26 January, a visitor claiming to be Hefeld's brother arrived at the hospital. He was promptly informed no one was to be allowed to see the prisoner without special permission from the police authorities. The man claimed he had only just heard of Hefeld's condition and had rushed overnight from Glasgow to see his brother.

The Special Services Department at Scotland Yard were alerted and the man was questioned. It was only after the initial interrogation that Inspector Hester arrived and he recognised the man as Johan Niderorst, a Swiss journalist who had written articles on revolutionary subjects for newspapers both abroad and in England. On being pressed by Hester, Niderorst admitted he had lied to obtain access to Hefeld as he had undertaken to obtain an exclusive interview with the prisoner for a local newspaper.

Niderorst was informed by the angry policeman that his explanation was not satisfactory and he was charged as 'a suspected person found on enclosed premises for an unlawful purpose'. Wasting police time may have been a more appropriate charge and when Niderorst appeared before the Tottenham Police Court, on 27 January, his plea of guilty was changed, under advisement, to not guilty.

Detective-Inspector Martin explained to the Court that he and Superintendent Jenkins had been called to the hospital and had interviewed the defendant. The prisoner had told them his name was Karl Hefeld and he resided in Glasgow. He had provided them with a full, though entirely fictitious, background to his 'Karl Hefeld' character, claiming he had; left his home in Riga fourteen years ago; been educated in France, Italy and Switzerland; come to Britain in 1903; studied English in Edinburgh and had initially made a living teaching languages.

The defendant had gone on to claim he was the brother of Paul Hefeld and that the two had resided together in Glasgow. He had then claimed Paul was a member of the Lettish Social Democratic Party. 'Karl' had stated categorically that he himself was not a member of any party and claimed he had been outraged by the crimes committed. He had gone on to reveal that his brother always carried a revolver because of a fear of being tracked by the Russian Secret Service.

'Karl' described himself as being self-employed, producing drawings to specification. He finished his elaborate tale by saying he had lived in Paris for three years but had preferred living in Glasgow (this statement alone should have triggered alarm bells).

Detective Inspector John McCarthy was then called and stated he had known the defendant for several years and recalled an occasion, four years earlier, when Niderorst had concocted a story about bombs being manufactured in Whitechapel. McCarthy opined that Niderorst was not an anarchist but a casual journalist and had not been at the hospital for illegal purposes.

Niderorst admitted he had gone to the hospital in the hope of obtaining a sensational exclusive interview with Hefeld. He had claimed to be Hefeld's brother because he had heard only close relatives would be granted access to the wounded man. He then claimed, unconvincingly, that he did not realise how serious the matter was. He apologised and was discharged with a reprimand.

The funerals of Police-Constable William Frederick Tyler and young Ralph Joscelyne were held together on 29 January 1909. Floral tributes arrived in huge numbers and a message of condolence from King Edward the Seventh was conveyed to the widow and family of the murdered policeman. Three thousand police officers joined the procession as it wound its way from the constable's residence in Arnold Road to the Abney Park Cemetery in Stoke Newington.

Up to half a million people were estimated to have lined the two-and-a-half-mile route. All local businesses were temporarily closed and flags were flown at half-mast. Behind the hearse bearing the coffins were two hearses containing wreaths, followed by six carriages to convey the mourners. The police guard of honour was joined by representatives from the Scots Guards, the Fire Brigade and the Tramways. The coffins were taken from the hearse and placed on two biers for the duration of a simple service held in the cemetery chapel. The constable and the child were then laid to rest in neighbouring graves.

In stark contrast, a secret burial was carried out by the parish authorities in Walthamstow Cemetery. A plain coffin, with a plate bearing the inscription 'Jacob, aged about thirty years' was interred in the general section of the cemetery.

On 1 February 1909, an update on Paul Hefeld's condition was released, describing him as 'progressing favourably'. Hefeld was being guarded around the clock by a team of six police officers on rotating shifts. He was said to be barely lucid and prone to making random wild statements.

On 2 February, Sir Albert De Rutzen issued the following statement regarding the public appeal on behalf of the widow of Police-Constable Tyler:-

'Owing to the generous response the public has made to my appeal on behalf of Police-Constable Tyler's widow, sufficient money has been received to meet the requirements of the case. The money received will, over the next few days, be placed in the hands of the Public Trustee. It is intended the interest from this fund shall be devoted to the widow for her life and at her death the principal sum will be paid over, as originally notified, to the Metropolitan and City Police Orphanage, so the widows and orphans of all police officers may derive benefit from the generosity of the public on this occasion.'

The fund had reached a total of £1,055 when Sir Albert issued his statement, it would go on to reach almost £1,220 before it was finally closed. Each person that donated, unless they chose to remain anonymous, was named in the newspapers.

Obviously feeling under some pressure, the Social Democratic Party of the Lettish Provinces issued a statement disclaiming any connection with Hefeld or Lepidus and expressing their regret at the perpetration of the crime.

11 February brought a fresh statement from the Prince of Wales Hospital, an announcement that Hefeld was now in a serious condition and it was thought his injuries may prove to be fatal.

The following day, it was revealed that Hefeld was due to have an operation and, even if the operation was successful, it would be at least a further three weeks before he would be in any condition to appear before a court.

Paul Hefeld died in the Prince of Wales Hospital on 12 February 1909 and the Inquest into his death took place four days later.

During the Inquest, Morris Sowermann, a local tobacconist, identified Hefeld as a man who had resided with him for a period of about three weeks. Hefeld had told Sowermann he was from Riga; was twenty-one-years-old; had been working since the age of fourteen; had arrived in Britain about one year ago and had come to Tottenham from Scotland.

Dr Frederick Shannon, the house surgeon at the Prince of Wales Hospital, stated that Hefeld was admitted on 23 January with a bullet wound in the side of his right eye. On the left side of the head was a further wound, where the bullet had passed through and exited. The root of the right eye had been fractured, but the eye itself was not injured. The doctor had found other, minor, wounds that Hefeld had incurred during the chase. Hefeld had, apparently, reacted well to treatment and his wounds had closed.

By 9 February, the situation had changed and Hefeld had contracted meningitis. It was decided that an operation would be necessary. The operation was carried out by Dr Carson and had initially appeared to have been successful. Shortly afterwards, however, the condition worsened and the patient died on 12 February.

Under direction from the Coroner, a verdict of *felo de se* was returned.

Detective Dixon and Police-Constables Nichol, Cater, Dewhurst and Eagles were all promoted to the rank of sergeant without the requirement for examination. Constables Newman and Ziething, who had not been in service long enough to be considered for promotion, were placed on the maximum pay rate for their rank. Financial rewards were paid to Sergeant Jowlett and Constables Blaydon, McKay, Lawrence, Willison and Frazer. Commendations were received by Superintendent Jenkins and Sub-Divisional-Inspector Large.

A further public subscription, including a Government Grant of £100 and a donation of £100 from the Carnegie Hero Fund, raised £698. This money was disbursed between the forty-six police officers and forty-two members of the public who had been involved in the incident. £30 was donated to the Prince of Wales Hospital and £15 to the Walthamstow Hospital.

Police-Constables Eagles, Dixon and Cater would later become recipients of the King's Police Medal for Gallantry, which was first instituted in July 1909. The medal could not, however, be awarded posthumously (although this rule was to change in 1977) so Police-Constable Tyler missed out on the honour.

This event, which would become known as 'The Tottenham Outrage', had been one of the first where the public had openly displayed such widespread backing for the police. The amounts raised in the public appeals and the numbers that attended the funeral procession of Police-Constable Tyler and Ralph Joscelyne were remarkable.

The King's Police Medal for Gallantry, first introduced to honour the policemen involved in ending 'The Tottenham Outrage', would be replaced in 1940 by the King's Police and Fire Services Medal, which would, in turn, be replaced by The Queen's Police Medal in 1954.

Amendments made to the Alien Act resulting from this incident and others would mean that, in future, any alien wishing to possess a firearm would require a permit which would have to be granted publicly in open court.

Power was given to Chiefs of Police whereby, in emergencies where a delay was likely to endanger life, they would have the authority to bypass the need for a warrant from the Justice and could issue orders for weapons searches directly to their subordinates.

Sadly, but perhaps unsurprisingly, the backlash against suspected anarchists would lead to a public fear of all immigrants. It would signal the beginning of a sharp rise in anti-Semitism.

5 THE GIRL WITH PRETTY FEET

In the year of 1934, the face of Europe was changing. Adolf Hitler's government signed a ten-year pact of non-aggression with Poland, while at the same time clearing the way within Germany to allow him to claim the position of Fuhrer. Right-wing protesters rioted in Paris in what would become a successful attempt to overthrow the leftist coalition government. The Austrian government issued a decree dissolving all political parties except the Fatherland Front. The Soviet Union extended its pacts of non-aggression with Poland and Finland, while simultaneously beginning a massive new armament program. The Dutch parliament granted emergency powers to control the activities of extremist political parties, which would ultimately fail in its bid to limit the growth within the country of the National Socialist Party.

A storm was clearly brewing.

Meanwhile, on the relatively sleepy south coast of the United Kingdom, the warm summer weather was about to unveil an unwelcome surprise. Brighton, a bustling and quirky seaside resort that had begun to garner a reputation as a destination for illicit weekend trysts and a haven for London gangsters, was about to hit the headlines.

Graham Greene would ensure the place gained worldwide recognition in his novel 'Brighton Rock', in 1938, but Brighton was destined to hit the headlines several years before that classic was published.

On Sunday 17 June 1934, at Brighton Railway Station, William Joseph Vinnicombe, a relief cloakroom porter with the Southern Railway Company, was disturbed by a pungent smell emanating from the Station's left-luggage office. Vinnicombe put his nose to the ground and traced the odour back to a brown canvas, double-locked suitcase. The suitcase itself was unremarkable and had no visible labelling. The contents, however, were to prove considerably more interesting.

Vinnicombe decided it would be advisable not to disturb the scene and set off to inform the railway policeman, Detective Bishop, of his find. Bishop, fearing the worst, was also wary of opening the rancid smelling luggage and in turn alerted the local Brighton Police.

Detective-Sergeant Percy Scales, of the Brighton Borough Police, responded to the call and prised open the suitcase. The railway employees had been right to be apprehensive, inside the suitcase were the rotting remains of a human being. When he had recovered from the shock, Scales decided that this was, literally, a case for Scotland Yard.

Chief Inspector Ronald Donaldson, a vastly experienced member of the Yard's Criminal Investigation Team, was assigned to the investigation and promptly set off for Brighton, accompanied by Detective-Sergeant Sorrell. Donaldson arrived to find the human remains to be the dismembered body of a woman. The head, arms and legs were all missing. Initial thoughts were the body was that of a woman aged between forty and forty-five years of age and about five-foot-two-inches in height.

The local Brighton Police examined the records they held on missing persons but were unable to find anyone who fitted the description of the dead woman. All train stations in the vicinity were alerted to the discovery of the torso in Brighton and were asked to check their left-luggage offices in the hope of locating the missing body parts.

On 18 June, a member of staff working in the cloakroom of King's Cross Station, London, had his attention drawn to a suitcase standing in a rack within the station's left luggage section. He perceived a peculiar odour escaping from within the suitcase and informed the Railway Police, who quickly alerted Scotland Yard. The Yard took possession of the offending item, which was found to contain a pair of legs and feet wrapped in pieces of brown paper. Records showed the suitcase had been deposited in the left-luggage department on 7 June.

In the meantime, the investigation in Brighton had uncovered that the suitcase containing the torso had been deposited at the Station on 6 June, Derby Day.

On 19 June, a post-mortem, shrouded in secrecy, was held by Sir Bernard Spilsbury, the Home Office pathologist. Following his work on the Crippen case in 1910 and the 'Brides in the Bath' murder in 1915, Sir Bernard was considered Britain's foremost pathologist. After examining the legs found at King's Cross, Spilsbury travelled to Brighton and was met on the outskirts of town by police officers who directed him to the mortuary.

Sir Bernard was accompanied by a police surgeon, Dr Pulling, and the pathologist of Sussex County Hospital, Dr Jaines. The gruelling post-mortem on the torso lasted for over three hours. It established that the woman was probably in her mid-twenties, around half the age she was initially thought to be and had been around five months pregnant at the time of her death. She had been not much taller than five-foot-three-inches, close enough to what had been previously thought A connection was made between the wrappings that had been tied around the body and those that had concealed the legs. It was considered likely that death had taken place no longer than three weeks earlier.

No identifying marks were found on the torso or legs. The torso had been covered in brown paper tied with a length of relatively new cord, approximately nineteen feet long. The cord was the type described in the trade as, two-pound jute, Venetian blind line.

The letters 'f-o-r-d' could be seen on the paper wrapped around the torso, but this was only part of what had originally been written, the rest was undecipherable.

A public appeal was made for information to assist in identifying the dead woman. Scotland Yard officers in Brighton and London, as well as a large body of county police officers, interviewed scores of people and collated thousands of reports based on the information they received.

Following a conference of Sussex police chiefs, a decision was taken to expand the search for the scene of the dismemberment to cover the whole of the county. Within hours of the conference ending, Detective-Sergeant Sorrell was embarking on a high-speed journey to a remote bungalow twenty miles outside Brighton. Having carried out a meticulous search of the building and surrounding area, Sorrell returned with a parcel wrapped in brown paper. He was soon on the road again and motoring towards the downs near Brighton Racecourse. When he arrived, he was faced with the unenviable task of searching through a manure heap. His search was rewarded by the uncovering of yet more brown wrapping paper.

Tips, of varying degrees of usefulness, were beginning to flood in from the public and on his return journey from the

Racecourse, Sorrell was asked to stop off and search through allotments in Wilson Avenue. There was a growing conviction among the police close to the case, that the dismemberment had been carried out somewhere in Sussex, probably in an isolated building within the coastal area.

Police issued a statement that the woman had painted toe-nails. This statement was soon retracted, presumably when someone with their eyes open looked at the body parts. A fuller description of the feet was issued and read, 'We wish to contradict a statement that the woman's toenails were painted. All that can be said is that there were no corns or other deformities on the feet. The toe-nails were well kept, short and evenly-cut not long before death.' This description would lead to some members of the press referring to the victim as 'The Girl with Pretty Feet.'

Meanwhile, the police continued their extensive search of the area, conducting hundreds of interviews with members of the public and visiting all local hotels and boarding-houses to speak to the transient guests within.

Scotland Yard announced they had compiled their most comprehensive list to date of missing women, a list that was believed to contain more than one thousand names. Since the investigation had begun, scores of new missing women had been reported to Scotland Yard and Brighton Police. These were carefree times indeed.

The Yard later announced their intention to release the list to the newspapers. It was decided to do this in stages, with those women whose descriptions were believed to be the closest fit to that of the victim being released first. The first list contained the details of ten missing women, all of whom had come from or were last seen near Brighton.

The list was accompanied by a police statement. 'The

following list of young women who have been reported missing and whose subsequent discovery has not been notified to the police is published in the hope the young women themselves, their relations, or anyone who can give definite information as to their whereabouts, will communicate immediately with New Scotland Yard. Any information will be treated as confidential.'

Three weeks into the investigation, Chief Inspector Donaldson was forced to admit he was no closer to being able to identify the woman whose dismembered body had been discovered in Brighton Railway Station.

Police officers had followed up on every piece of information provided to them by the public, had spoken to every person brought to their attention and had issued updated descriptions of both the woman and the trunk in which she had been discovered. Following a surprisingly high success rate in the tracing of the missing women detailed in the first of the lists they had issued, the police issued a second and third list of missing women. More than half of the women were traced within twenty-four hours.

Donaldson expressed his surprise at how quickly many of the women, all of whom had been officially classified as 'missing persons', were being located. He confirmed new lists would continue to be circulated.

One positive line of inquiry being pursued had followed receipt of information regarding a man who had been seen travelling from Dartford to Brighton, via London Bridge, on Derby Day, with a trunk like the one in which the body had been found. 'The Man from Dartford' was described as 'Aged thirty-five; between five-foot-six and five-foot-eight; medium build; clean shaven and wearing a raincoat and cap.'

Just when it looked like it had hit the buffers, the investigation veered crazily down a side-track.

During extensive police searches, the body of a second woman was discovered in a trunk in a room in Kemp Street, Brighton. Although the obvious initial conclusion was that the two murders were related, Scotland Yard quickly dismissed the idea and 'Brighton Trunk Crime Number 2' would follow its own separate investigative route (which is covered in detail in the next story, 'The Dancing Waiter').

The circulation of the names of missing women continued into July and one individual name, Daisy Johnson, aged twenty-four, was issued nationwide accompanied by a photograph. This woman too was quickly traced and found to be alive and well.

Scotland Yard continued to follow-up on every piece of information they received and 'digging sites' began appearing around Brighton, but still, the police had no success in locating the missing body parts.

An updated description of the victim's feet was issued, the unhealthy obsession with the feet clearly being due to the complete lack of any other distinguishing features. Misleading reports had somehow been circulated indicating that the second toe on each of the woman's feet was larger than the big toe. This information was corrected and all the toes were described as well-formed and possibly longer than usual, but in no way considered abnormal.

Following the request for information from the public, over six thousand letters had been received at Brighton Police Station alone.

After discovering a trunk containing women's clothing and a pair of shoes in a boarding-house on the outskirts of Brighton, police announced they urgently required to speak to the writer of one of the letters they had received. The letter had been signed with the nom de plume '8334'. The letter's author visited Scotland Yard the following day and was interviewed by Detective Inspector Rees, who had been placed in charge of enquiries in London. '8334' added to the information he had provided in the letter and this information was quickly passed to Chief Inspector Donaldson with a request for the new information to be acted upon with the greatest urgency. In keeping with the appeal issued for him to come forward, every precaution was taken to prevent the identity of '8334' becoming known.

A new line of enquiry was opened as result of the information provided by '8334' and a further systematic check of cafes, bungalows and boarding-houses was carried out. On this round of enquiries, police asked questions regarding a fair-haired woman who had come from London and had been in Brighton during May. The name of the woman, though known to the police, was withheld. The woman was described as 'of good social standing' but had been seen on many occasions in places where dancing went on into the early hours.

The investigation spread into London's theatre district, where a number of chorus girls had been reported as being missing after having arrived in the Capital with various travelling shows.

The pressure was beginning to take its toll and Detective Inspector Rees was rushed to the hospital to be looked at by specialists. Rees, a vastly experienced officer, around forty years old, had been involved in many visits to Brighton as well as overseeing coordination of the London enquiries.

Chief Inspector Donaldson was dealing directly with all the most promising leads emanating from Brighton. The lists of missing women were continuing to be circulated, appeals for various anonymous correspondents to come forward were being issued and 'The Man from Dartford' was still being sought as the month of July came to an end.

August 1934 arrived with two new pieces of correspondence now exercising the attention of Scotland Yard. The first had been signed 'Pro Bono Publico' and hand-writing experts offered that the letter had been written by a man. The second letter was anonymous and experts believed it had been written by a woman. Scotland Yard made several attempts to encourage the woman to come forward to expand on the information she had provided in the letter, but there was a general feeling among the policemen that the woman's subsequent silence was due to fear of recrimination from a party afraid of being incriminated by her testimony.

Although there was no let-up in the police enquiries into the murder, there was a growing fear the investigations were reaching a position of stalemate. Unless a breakthrough came soon, there was a possibility the Scotland Yard officers would be withdrawn from the case, leaving the matter in the hands of local police. Chief Inspector Donaldson transferred his headquarters in Brighton to a room in the magnificent Royal Pavilion, a former royal residence that had been sold to the town in 1850. There, he buried himself among the fresh deluge of letters that had been received from the public. Donaldson appealed for patience, pointing out that Scotland Yard had a history of solving crimes involving many months of painstaking police work.

Day fifty of the investigation saw the start of a search for a tattooed sailor who had been reported missing from his ship and had not been seen for almost two months. The man's name contained the letters 'f-o-r-d' within it, thus tying it to the suitcase discovered in Brighton. The sailor also fitted the description the police had received of a man who had been seen on many occasions in the company of a young Brighton woman who had been reported missing. Police forces throughout the country were provided with a description. The tattooed seaman was traced to Trowbridge but, disappointingly, the information he provided did not assist in driving things forward.

By the beginning of September, the number of letters received from the public had doubled to twelve thousand and Donaldson confirmed that every clue suggested within the correspondence had been followed up.

The newspapers were beginning to describe the crime as the 'perfect murder'. Some reporters were expressing the view the perpetrator had learned from the mistakes that had brought to justice others who had dismembered the bodies of their victims. Donaldson, not willing to buy into this theory, was keen to state his belief the murder had likely been 'perfect' by accident rather than by design.

It certainly could be argued that the 'perfect murder' would have meant the perpetrator having as much success in hiding the whereabouts of the torso and legs as they'd had with the head and arms. The discovery of the two suitcases containing body parts might suggest Donaldson was closer to the truth in his assessment that the culprit had been blessed with some degree of luck in evading capture.

On 5 September, fresh impetus was brought to the case and Chief Constable Horwell, head of the Criminal Investigation Department at Scotland Yard, arrived in Brighton. The increased activity resulted from the discovery of a suitcase and attaché case within the unclaimed luggage office of the Southdown Motor Company's headquarters in Brighton. The baggage had been transferred to Brighton after the owner had failed to reclaim them from an office in Lewes, the county town of East Sussex.

Examination of the contents of the cases revealed several photographs of a middle-aged woman, together with some women's underclothing and some letters addressed 'Dear Florrie'. Scotland Yard's handwriting experts examined the letters found in the case and compared them with correspondence already in their possession.

The letters helped detectives to connect the luggage to the reported disappearance of a young woman from Newick, a village and civil parish in the Lewes District. Florrie was known to have worked as a servant on a farm in Newick. She was positively identified as the person who had deposited the two cases at the luggage office of the Southdown Company at Lewes and it was known she had not been seen in the village since that day.

Detectives were sent, post-haste, from Brighton to Newick. Other officers, armed with a full description, were dispatched to locate the man police believed had written the letters. On 6 September, Donaldson reported that the police had traced and interviewed Florrie Annie Martin, the owner of the two suitcases, at the home of a relative living a few miles from Lewes.

Scotland Yard issued a renewed request to all railway companies, asking that they check again for any bags or parcels that had been in their possession for an unusual length of time. The new search resulted in the discovery of a bag, containing papers, in the cloakroom of an Underground station in North London. The papers appeared to have a connection with the investigation.

The information contained in the papers led Donaldson to interview a woman who was currently serving a sentence in a London Prison. The story she told the policeman at first appeared to have provided a clue as to the disposal of the missing head. After following up the lead and failing to find anything to corroborate the woman's statement, the Chief Inspector was forced to admit that the month of September had ended with the investigation having headed down another dead-end street.

October began with two new high-profile leads. The continuing information being provided by the public led to extensive enquiries about two further women reported as missing, one in London and one on the South Coast.

A statement provided to the police by a friend of one of the missing women claimed she had been working in Weymouth, a seaside town in Dorset, when she had become friendly with a man of foreign nationality. The friend said the woman had later moved to the Sussex Coast in the company of the mysterious foreigner and had not been heard from since. The second missing woman was reported to have lived in the Brighton area and had been seen with a foreign-looking man in May, but had not been seen or heard of since that time.

If you were wishing to avoid suspicion, this was clearly not a good time to be a 'foreign-looking' gentleman in Southern England, especially if you were seen at any time in the company of young English women.

On 19 October, it was decided that the legs and feet discovered in London should be moved from their present location, in Paddington Mortuary, to be held in Brighton pending a Public Inquiry into the murder.

November saw the retirement of an officer who had been involved in the early investigations in Brighton, Chief Inspector Bowden, Head of Hove Criminal Investigation Department. Bowden had his own thoughts on where he believed the case currently stood and couldn't resist revealing them to the press. He informed the reporters that the identity of the culprit was known to the police, but they did not have sufficient evidence to warrant an arrest. Bowden said, somewhat cryptically, he was convinced the investigation may have followed an entirely different course if the suitcase containing the torso had been discovered earlier.

Donaldson, unimpressed by his colleague's statement, moved quickly to dampen speculation. Donaldson said a more accurate assessment of the position would be that the police had grave suspicions but, while they had no doubt these suspicions were well founded, they had insufficient evidence to justify an arrest. On reflection, the statement really didn't do much to deter speculation.

The man that is now known to be the subject of the Chief Inspector's grave suspicions was Dr Edward Seys Massiah of Brunswick Square, Hove.

Massiah, a man of mixed-race, ran a medical practice offering discreet abortion services, an illegal activity at the time. Donaldson considered Massiah to be a prime suspect but was having difficulty in uncovering any concrete evidence to link the doctor directly to the case. Although he was unable to pin anything on the doctor, the dearth of other leading suspects pushed Donaldson into asking the local Hove police to keep a close eye on Massiah's movements.

In a rash attempt to grab the credit for solving the case, an over-eager, high-ranking, Hove police officer ignored the watching brief Donaldson had ordered. The policeman turned up at Massiah's practice without backup and during a face-to-face confrontation, accused the doctor of being directly involved in the murder of the dismembered female.

Massiah's reaction to the accusation came as a complete shock to the open-mouthed policeman. Rather than showing any signs of concern, the doctor calmly reached across his desk and picked up his pen and notepad. Messiah then drew up a list of names and addresses which he pushed into the face of the startled policeman. The list contained the names and addresses of several of the most prominent people in the county. We can only presume, as the policeman surely did, the doctor had drawn up a list of high-profile people who had made use of, or at least had knowledge of, the illegal services provided by the doctor. It soon dawned on the police officer that he had made a huge mistake in approaching Messiah without the evidence required to back up his accusations. It was clear to him he had blown the case by letting the cat out of the bag.

It was some considerable time later that Chief Inspector Donaldson was made aware of what had happened in Hove. To add insult to injury, the message did not come in the form of an apology, but in the shape of a direct warning to 'lay off Massiah'. The concerns of those in high places appeared to have trumped the suspicions of the Scotland Yard Chief Inspector.

Now fully armed with the knowledge he was under suspicion, Massiah left Hove and opened a practice in London. It would take the death of another woman, during a botched illegal abortion at his London practice, to encourage Messiah to flee justice by shipping out of England altogether. The abortionist set sail for Trinidad, where he would live out the remainder of his life as a free man in the sunny city of Port of Spain.

On 19 November, the shooting of a police officer in London resulted in Chief Inspector Donaldson's removal from the Brighton murder case and re-assignment to take charge of the investigation into the London shooting. Although the shooting of a policeman was a high-profile, top-priority matter, this was perhaps the clearest indication yet that the Brighton murder case was destined to remain officially unsolved.

On 20 February 1935, the much-delayed Inquest into the death of 'The Girl with Pretty Feet' was held. The jury returned an Open Verdict.

The Coroner read the following extracts from the post-mortem report of Sir Bernard Spilsbury:-

'The body was that of a well-nourished woman. In the neck, the line of division passed through the fifth cervical vertebrae. The arms had been severed a short distance below the shoulders, the right at a lower level than the left. The legs had been severed a short distance below the hips, the left leg at a lower level than the right.

On 20 June, I made a post-mortem examination of two human lower limbs found in a box at King's Cross Station. The limbs formed an exact pair. The limbs had been separated from the trunk through the upper part of the thighs and each limb was further divided at the knee. There were no corns, bunions or other deformities on the feet.

The torso found at Brighton and the lower limbs found at King's Cross are parts of the same body, that of a young woman about twenty-five years of age. She was well developed but was not stout and was about five-foot-three-inches in height. She appears to have been a healthy woman. No disease was found in her body and the structure of her leg bones suggest she led an active life and there was probably no history of serious illness in childhood. The thighs, legs and feet are perfectly clean and like the trunk, show no marks or injury.

I found no natural disease to account for death. There was no indication of poisoning and there were no marks of violence on the body or lower limbs. I am, therefore, unable to state the cause of death.'

When he was asked for his views by the Coroner, a weary Chief Inspector Donaldson stated that no useful purpose would be served by keeping the Inquiry open.

Because of the difficulty they had experienced in their attempt to identify the woman whose dismembered body had been discovered at Brighton Railway Station, Scotland Yard revealed they would be revising their system for the registration of missing persons. In many of the cases the police had pursued, women who were still registered as missing had been traced and found to be alive and well. Neither the women, their relatives nor friends had deemed it necessary to inform the police of their whereabouts if they had resurfaced after their initial disappearance had been reported. Beyond the printing and circulation of descriptions, authorities took no further action on their lists of missing persons unless there was a reason to expect foul play.

A decision was made to implement a new central alphabetical index that would be cross-referenced with the dates on which people were reported missing. Police forces would be expected to report any fresh information they received regarding the individuals on the list to enable it to be maintained and updated at the very earliest opportunity.

This had been the first occasion on which the police had utilised the assistance of the public on such a grand scale. Many lessons, on both the merits and drawbacks of this fresh approach, were to be learned from the case.

Newspapers around the country had been provided with more detail than ever before on an active investigation. The declared intention of Scotland Yard had been to recruit the public as 'detectives' on the case. The sheer volume of the information provided by the public had, however, taken officers by surprise and the investigation, while failing to reach a successful conclusion, had certainly provided Scotland Yard with plenty food for thought.

6 THE DANCING WAITER

As we now know, the case of 'The Girl with Pretty Feet' ended in failure from the police perspective. During that case, the police had discovered, in a house in Brighton, the trunk that had set in motion the 'Brighton Trunk Murder No.2' investigation. The fact they had an immediate description of their chief suspect available to issue, meant hopes were high that this new case could be brought to an early and successful conclusion.

The search of the properties surrounding Brighton Railway Station triggered by the discovery of a woman's torso in the left luggage department, had, on 15 July 1934, led the police to number 52 Kemp Street.

An all too familiar smell greeted the police officers as they entered the basement flat. They discovered a large black trunk, bound up with a cord. The policemen cut the cord and opened the lid of the trunk to reveal a dirty blood-stained overcoat, a blanket, some women's clothing and, peeking out beneath these, the head and arm of a human being. The trunk was quickly removed to the local mortuary, where it was found to contain a woman's body with a scarf wrapped around the neck.

On 17 July, police announced they had identified the murdered woman as forty-two-year-old Violet Saunders.

Sir Bernard Spilsbury was called in to examine the body. The badly decomposed body was that of a well-nourished woman. There were signs that were usually present after a full-term pregnancy. On the scalp were what appeared to be bruises caused shortly before death. Beneath a bruise on the right side of the head was a large depressed fracture of the skull, extending downwards. There was also a short crack fissured fracture of the skull, extending upwards from the upper edge of the depressed fracture. The fractures, in Spilsbury's opinion, had been produced by a violent blow from a blunt object and had caused death from shock.

There were also two small bruises behind the left ear, indicating to Spilsbury that the woman had been lying upon a hard surface at the time the violent blow had been struck and the skull fractured. A minute trace of morphine was discovered, indicating the woman had taken more than a medicinal dose. Whilst such a dose might result in drowsiness or unconsciousness, Spilsbury's opinion was that this had made no difference to the cause of death.

It was Spilsbury's view the fracture of the skull may have been caused by a blow from a hammer. He considered a fall from a standing position could not possibly have resulted in the fracture and only a fall from fifteen to twenty feet could have caused similar damage.

The mother of Violet Saunders was brought to Brighton from London and she positively identified the body being held in the borough mortuary as her daughter's.

The chief suspect was revealed to be a man named Tony Mancini who, until only hours before the discovery of the body, had been renting the flat in Kemp Street. A description was quickly issued to all local police stations.

Mancini surfaced in Stepney, London, on 15 July. There, he met up with a young and impressionable seventeen-year-old girl named Doris Saville and the topic of conversation between the two soon took on a sinister tone. Saville heard from Mancini that he had been implicated in a murder, of which, he claimed, he was entirely innocent. He then attempted to involve the girl in a concocted story he hoped would clear him.

The story would be that Mancini and Saville had met on the beach in Brighton at the end of May. They were to have visited a woman at 44 Park Crescent. Following the visit, they would claim to have left the woman alone, as she had told them she was expecting three male visitors. After going for a walk, they would claim to have returned to the flat to find the woman had been murdered and the three men had gone. Mancini told Saville he just wanted someone to stand beside him in court if he should be put up for murder.

As first dates go, this one would certainly be up there among the strangest.

Having beguiled the girl with his tale, Mancini took a room at the Salvation Army hostel in Poplar, under the name Swinley. The next morning, he met up with a man named Isaac Smith and spent the rest of the day in his company.

Mancini pledged his trousers, overcoat and two shirts to obtain money which he planned to use to go to Cardiff, where he hoped to hire a boat.

At around 1:15am on 17 April, Mancini was spotted stumbling along the road between London and Maidstone by two Metropolitan Police officers. The policemen stopped him to ask where he was going, to which he replied, 'Maidstone.' One of the officers noted he bore a striking resemblance to the suspect whose description had been circulated in connection with the recent murder in Brighton.

The policemen drove Mancini back to the police-station in Lee Road. During the journey, Mancini admitted, 'Yes, I am the man, but I did not murder her. I would not even cut her hand. She has been keeping me for months.' When he was formally charged, Mancini's only comment was, 'All I can say is, I am not guilty.'

The police officers phoned Chief Inspector Donaldson in Brighton. Donaldson and Detective Sergeant Sorrell set off immediately, arriving at Lee Road Police Station at around 5am. After satisfying themselves they had their man, they conveyed the prisoner to Brighton Town Hall, via Scotland Yard, to avoid the crowds already beginning to assemble outside the police station in Brighton, as news of an arrest began to break.

The news-hungry press was fed an official statement by Chief Inspector Donaldson. 'Regarding the offence described as Brighton Trunk Murder No. 2, Jack Notyre has now been charged with the wilful murder of Violet Saunders, known as Violet Kaye, or Violet Watson. He will appear at Brighton Police Court tomorrow morning. The Inquest on Violet Saunders will be opened tomorrow at 12 o'clock.'

Already, a bewildering number of names were beginning to appear in connection with the murder, given there were only two people involved, but this would prove to be only the tip of the iceberg. Jack Notyre, generally known at the time as Tony Mancini, but born Cecil Lois England and at various stages also known as Tony English, Hyman Gold, Luigi Pirelli or Toni Luigi, was a twenty-six-year-old waiter, ballroom dancer (in both the literal and cockney rhyming-slang senses), ex boxing-booth pugilist, Lothario, London mob enforcer, fantasist and pimp.

Violet Saunders, nee Watts, also known as Violet Kaye or Violet Watson, was a forty-two-year-old waitress and had at one time performed as a professional chorus dancer. She was also a drunk, drug user and prostitute. In 1932 and through part of 1933, Saunders had toured on stage with a man named Kay Fredericks and they had performed under the stage-name Kay and Kaye.

Notyre had first met Saunders in London when she was using the name, Violet Kaye. They had moved to Brighton sometime in the autumn of 1933. On 19 March 1934, the couple, under the name Mr and Mrs Watson, moved into a basement flat at 44 Park Crescent. Notyre informed the landlord, Mr Snuggs, his occupation was as a gentleman's clothes presser. The flat consisted of three rooms, a living room, a bedroom and a kitchen.

A frequent visitor to the flat was a man called Charles Moores, who was referred to by the couple as 'uncle'. Moores would generally arrive in a chauffeur-driven car. His last known visit to the flat was on 4 May and later that evening he was, intriguingly, whisked off to Brighton Mental Infirmary at Haywards Heath. An interesting visitor indeed.

Notyre gained employment as a handyman and waiter at a place called the Skylark Cafe in Brighton on 5 May. The following week was the last time Violet Saunders was seen alive. She was seen on 7 May by Mr Snuggs, who did not see her again after that day. She was also seen at the Skylark Cafe, between 2:30 and 3pm on 10 May, by a woman who worked in the cafe.

Florence Attrill had overhead Notyre and Saunders arguing in the café. The fact the argument had been about her may have helped to grab the woman's attention. Notyre, at one stage, had turned to Attrill and told her to pay no attention to the argument as Violet was simply jealous.

Later that same day, a man who had been employed as a driver for Mr Moores called at 44 Park Crescent. Saunders answered the door and appeared to the man to be in a state of distress, seemingly nervous, with her hands and face twitching. The driver's layman's opinion was that she was under the influence of drugs. The driver was thought to be the last person to have seen Saunders alive.

Violet Saunders had a sister, Olive Watts, who lived in New Kent Road, London. Mrs Watts had planned a holiday, staying with her sister in Brighton, which was due to begin on 14 May. On 11 May, she was somewhat surprised to receive a telegram which read, 'GOING ABROAD. GOOD JOB. SAIL SUNDAY. WILL WRITE. VI.'

The telegram, set out in printed capitals, had been handed in at the head post office in Brighton at about 9am on 11 May, though post office officials would later be unable to say who had handed it in. Notyre was known to be accustomed to producing menu cards for the Skylark Cafe in similarly printed capitals. A leading handwriting expert would later claim the printing on the telegram and that used on the café's menus bore such a striking resemblance to each other as to lead to the conclusion the telegram was written by the same hand that had written the menu cards at the cafe.

On 11 May, Notyre took Miss Attrill to one of the local dance halls. He explained to the woman that Violet had gone to Paris. After the dancing, Notyre took Attrill back to his flat in Park Crescent, where he handed her a green costume and fawn hat. The items had been purchased by Notyre from a credit draper on 14 April and had both been worn, witnesses would later confirm, by Violet Saunders. Notyre also gave the woman a black coat, explaining that Violet had been unable to fit the clothes into her case. He had, he said, promised to send the clothes on to her, but had subsequently changed his mind.

Attrill noticed there were no bedclothes in the flat, Notyre claiming to have given them away, but there was a pair of woman's slippers under the bed. Notyre said Violet had bought new slippers to go away with and had left the old ones behind.

Shortly thereafter, Notyre went to Brighton Market and purchased a large black trunk with a tray on the inside and straps on the outside. It would be within this trunk the body of Violet Saunders would be discovered some two months later.

Notyre carried on working at the Skylark Cafe and it was there he crossed paths with Mr and Mrs Bernard, of 52 Kemp Street. The couple were regular customers at the cafe and on 6 May, they left cards behind advertising rooms to let in their household. When Mr and Mrs Bernard returned to the cafe the following week, Notyre informed told them he would be interested in becoming their tenant. The couple were happy with this arrangement and Notyre intimated he would bring his luggage to the property the following morning.

Next morning, at around 7:30am on 14 May, Notyre duly arrived, pulling his luggage, which included a large trunk, on a hand-cart. He told the couple his wife had gone to France with Charles Moores. Notyre said he had gone to London to visit his parents, expecting to find his wife there, but instead had found a letter stating she had gone off with Moores.

The property was located not far from Brighton Railway Station and Notyre moved into the tiny room in the basement, which contained two beds.

Notyre was known to frequent an amusement arcade called Aladdin's Cave, near Brighton Pier, where he would regale the people he met there with a variety of versions of his breakup with Saunders. Joyce Golding was told he had left Violet because of her continual nagging, adding that he hoped she would never come back as he did not want her following him in the streets shouting names at him. A woman named Gordon and a woman named Summers were both told Violet had gone to Montmartre in Paris and a man named Charteris was told she had left for Paris to become a bookmaker.

Other regulars in Aladdin's Cave spoke of Notyre telling them of having trouble with his 'missus' and of having dished out the biggest hiding she'd had in her life before she had packed her bags overnight and blown town. He had also offered his sage advice on the best way to deal with a troublesome woman, saying, 'What is the good of knocking a woman about with your fists? You only hurt yourself. You should hit them with a hammer, same as I did, and slosh her up,' emphasising his point by striking the palm of one hand with his fist.

Each night, Notyre would return to the flat in Kemp Street, where he would lie sleeping a few feet away from the trunk in which Violet Saunders' doubled-up body lay.

On occasions, other people would share the room with Notyre and would comment on the strange smell that seemed to hover in the air. Notyre would explain it in a variety of ways. He told one woman that someone had died in the room and it had been disinfected, but because the landlady never opened the window during the day the smell would not go away.

One morning, when looking to clean the room, Mrs Bernard was horrified to see a strange fluid oozing from the trunk. She set off for the Skylark Cafe to notify Notyre, who said it was French polish and that he would attend to it. That night the fluid was cleared up and a sack was placed under the trunk.

On the evening of 14 July, Notyre visited Sherry's

Dancehall and spent time in the company of a dance instructress, Joan Tinn, with whom he was acquainted. Notyre told the woman he was heading to London and when he did, Kemp Street, in fact, the whole of Brighton, would become famous. He told the woman he had used up all his father's money and was returning to London to see his father and 'some of the boys'.

On his way out of the dancehall, Notyre stumbled upon two friends and remained in their company for the rest of the night. As he was explaining to the men that he was going to London, Notyre saw one of the men was carrying a card from the local dog track. Asking to borrow it, he explained that should he be stopped at the other end of his journey, he would show the card and claim to have been at the dogs. The two men accompanied Notyre to the flat in Kemp Street where, ignoring the worsening stench, he picked up some personal items.

All three men then headed to Brighton Station, where Notyre inquired about the time of the next train to London. As there was going to be a while to wait, they spent some time in an all-night cafe before travelling to Preston Park Station, from where Notyre would be catching the train. As they waited on the platform, Notyre, somewhat mysteriously, informed the two men that a lot was going to be said in the news about Kemp Street and his picture would soon be appearing in the papers. With that, he boarded the train for London.

The trial of Jack Notyre, that being the name he was charged under despite it being one of his many aliases, began, before Justice Branson, at the Sussex Assizes in Lewes on 11 December 1934.

Mr Cassels and Mr Quentin Hogg appeared for the prosecution and Mr Norman Birkett, Mr John Flowers and Mr Eric Neve for the defence. The jury was entirely made up of men. Public interest was intense and the number of applications for tickets far exceeded the one hundred places available in the gallery.

After the Judge took his seat, the Clerk of Court called for Notyre to be brought up. He then read the charge. 'Jack Notyre, you are charged that you, between the 10th and 15th day of May of this year, at Brighton, murdered Violet Saunders. How say you, are you guilty or not guilty?'

As silence descended upon the courtroom, Notyre seemed to struggle to get the words out before, in a barely audible voice, he said, 'I am not.........' Seemingly unable to complete the sentence, Notyre was prompted again by a now irritated Clerk of Court before, finally, managing to utter the words, 'I am not guilty.'

Cassels opened for the prosecution and relayed to the jury the details of the body in the trunk, the visitors to the flat, the last sightings of Violet Saunders, Notyre's explanations of her disappearance, the discovery of the trunk and the prisoner's subsequent arrest.

Moving on, the prosecutor explained that there were two cupboards in the bedroom at 44 Park Crescent and signs of blood and fibres from the clothing found in the trunk had been discovered in one of them. The conclusion of the prosecution was that before it had been doubled-up in the black trunk, the woman's body had been hidden in the cupboard. The next tenants to lease the flat had found the tray that had been in the black trunk when Notyre had purchased it at Brighton Market. Cassels then revealed Dr Roche Lynch had examined the prisoners clothing and had found traces of human blood on three of his shirts and two pairs of his trousers.

Concluding his opening statement, Cassels said it was the submission of the prosecution that Violet Saunders had been murdered sometime between 10 May and 15 May, most probably on 10 May. He claimed the evidence, together with Notyre's conduct and his conversations after that time, irresistibly led to the conclusion the prisoner had been the person who had murdered Violet Saunders. With that, the first witnesses were called.

Henry Sidney Snuggs, who described himself as a retired ship's carpenter and now a motor driver, was first up. Snuggs said he had let the basement of his house to a couple he had known as Mr and Mrs Watson, though he now confirmed the man had been the prisoner, Jack Notyre.

Notyre had told Snuggs he was employed as a clothes presser. Snuggs was of the view the couple were very friendly and recalled they had been visited on several occasions by an elderly visitor they had said was 'Mrs Watson's' uncle. In reply to a question from Cassels, Snuggs claimed it was untrue to say there were always men coming to the flat at night. The last time Snuggs had seen 'Mrs Watson' alive had been on 7 May, when she had paid the rent on the flat.

On 14 May, Snuggs had seen Notyre with another woman, whom he introduced as his sister. Notyre had told Snuggs his wife had left him and that he would, therefore, be giving up the tenancy of the flat, claiming he could not live there alone. Adding that his wife had gone to France, Notyre arranged to collect his furniture the following day.

Under cross-examination by Mr Birkett, Snuggs said he had only seen a man going down to the basement with a woman on one occasion, sometime towards the end of April.

The man was described as 'rather tall and wearing a trilby hat'. The man had stayed for about half an hour, sometime between 10 and 11pm.

The witness said he had also seen the man called Charles Moores, who was referred to as 'uncle' by 'Mrs Watson'. Moores always arrived by car, though he would never be seen driving himself. Snuggs denied ever having seen two men known as 'Darky' and 'Hoppy'.

Evidence was then taken regarding Notyre's purchase of a dark trunk at Brighton Market. This was followed by testimony from Thomas Edwin Capelin, who had, on 15th or 16th May, gone to Park Crescent to assist Notyre with moving his luggage to Kemp Street. Capelin said the largest item of luggage had been the black trunk, which he confirmed looked like the one on display in Court as evidence. Adding that the trunk had been very heavy, Capelin confirmed he would have been unable to carry it by himself.

The next witness to be called was Thomas Richard Kerslake, a car driver from Franklin Road, Brighton. Kerslake said he had, on several occasions, driven a bookmaker named Charles Moores. On three of these occasions, he had driven Moores to the property at 44 Park Street and had watched as Moores had gone down to the basement. Kerslake revealed Moores had been taken to a mental institution sometime around 5 May.

The witness then stated that he himself had visited 44 Park Street on 10 May and had spoken to the woman in the basement. She had appeared to be in an excited, nervous, shaky condition and looked as if she may have been drinking. That was the last time he had seen the woman.

Questioned by Cassels, Kerslake confirmed Moores could not have visited Kemp Street on 10 May as he was still institutionalised. Cross-examined by Birkett, Kerslake confirmed Moores had since been released from the mental institution. Kerslake also revealed that, as he had walked away from the basement flat on 10 May, he'd seen another man go down the steps.

Next up was Turnbull Van Meusen, an officer at Brighton Hospital. Van Meusen said Charles Moores had been admitted to Brighton Hospital under a three-day mental health order on 4 May. Moores had been certified as being of unsound mind and had been in various institutions between 4 May and his final release on 30 October. Asked by Cassels to clarify what constituted a three-day order, Van Meusen replied it was notice given so a person could be kept under control until the question of his certification could be determined. Van Meusen declared he had taken the initiative in the matter and had thought it necessary on safety grounds, though he clarified there was no record of Moores becoming violent.

George and Ellen Barnard, the current occupiers of the property in Kemp Street, were the last witnesses to be called on day one of the trial and both testified that Notyre had appeared to them to be an exemplary tenant.

With that, the trial was adjourned for the day.

The trial resumed on 12 December.

The first major witness called was Elizabeth Attrill, a waitress who had been employed at the Skylark Cafe during the period Notyre had worked there.

Attrill revealed she had met with Notyre on 10 May, when he had informed her Violet Saunders had left him and gone off to Paris. Shortly thereafter, Attrill had moved into the flat in Park Crescent and had remained there for about a fortnight. During that period, Attrill had washed some of the prisoner's clothing and had noticed bloodstains on one of his shirts. Notyre had explained this away by claiming to have cut himself whilst shaving.

Another waitress, Joyce Golding, was called and told the Court she had known Notyre, under his Tony Mancini alias, for about six years. Just prior to Christmas 1933, she had met the prisoner and he had told her he'd quarrelled with Violet over a visit from her former dancing partner, Kay Fredericks.

Golding had next seen the prisoner in May 1934 at Aladdin's Cave, near Brighton Pier, and she'd seen him frequently over June and July of that year. Notyre had told her Violet had gone to Montmartre on a two-year contract and he'd suggested Golding move in with him.

When Birkett, during cross-examination, put it to Golding that it was a deliberate lie to say the prisoner had asked her to move in with him, she replied, 'He invited me for the simple reason that he knew what I really was.'

The next witness called was John James Cochrane, an attendant at the skittles stall in Aladdin's Cave. Cochrane said he had met Notyre on the evening before the Brighton Races began in June. The prisoner had told him he'd had a tiff with his 'missus' and had given her the biggest hiding she'd had in her life.

The prisoner had then told Cochrane Saunders was not, in fact, his wife but was a prostitute he had lived with and kept for three years (which was very much a distortion of the truth regarding which one lived off the other's earnings). Notyre had finished by saying he did not expect to see Saunders again as, when he had got up in the morning, she had blown town.

George Boxall, a sanitary engineer, testified next and

claimed to have overheard Notyre, in where else but Aladdin's Cave, say, 'What is the good of knocking a woman about with your fists? You only hurt yourself. You should hit them with a hammer, same as I did, and slosh her up.'

Next in the line of witnesses with unusual jobs was showman's manager, Albert Edward Pitman. The witness had met Notyre in the Skylark Cafe and had spent the night sleeping in one of the made-up beds in the room in Kemp Street, while the prisoner slept in the other.

Pitman said he had noticed a strange smell lingering in the room. When he'd raised this with Notyre, he'd been told that somebody who had occupied the room had recently died from tuberculosis and the landlady had since had the room disinfected.

Dancing instructress Joan Tinn then gave her testimony, outlining Notyre's remarks to her that Kemp Street and Brighton were about to become famous.

The next witness to be called was Dr Roche Lynch, Senior Official Analyst to the Home Office, who was to give evidence regarding tests he had carried out on a number of exhibits relating to the case.

The first item Lynch was handed was a hammer-head. The analyst confirmed no traces of blood had been found on the hammer-head, which had been coated in a fine ash when he had first examined it, leaving him with the impression it had been heated in a fire. The effects of the fire would, Lynch contended, have destroyed any blood marks that may have been on the hammer head.

Moving on to various human organs handed to him, the analyst said he had detected unquantifiable traces of morphine. Considering the advanced state of decomposition of the organs, the fact the Doctor had found any traces of morphine indicated to him that a quantity had been taken that was distinctly greater than any medicinal dose. The result of taking such a dose would, Lynch said, be a feeling of sleepiness followed by deep sleep and, in all likelihood, unconsciousness.

Cassels asked the analyst whether he would have expected to find a similar quantity of morphine if the woman had been an addict. Lynch replied that in such circumstances, he would not have expected to have found any trace of morphine. When cross-examined by Birkett, Lynch clarified that in the case of addicts, morphine was so quickly destroyed in the body that it was only with the greatest of difficulty one would find it at all. The analyst stated firmly that traces of morphine would not be found in the decomposed body of an addict.

Next, questioned about bloodstains found on a shirt, Lynch stated that human blood was divided into four groups and every member of the public fell into one of these groups. Its value in criminal investigations, the doctor continued, was that if an alleged murderer had blood on his clothing and the group of that blood matched that of the victim but was different from his own group, he naturally would require to provide an explanation.

In this case, Lynch said, with each of the articles of clothing he had examined, it had been impossible to distinguish the group to which the blood spots had belonged. Anti-climactically, Lynch also admitted that owing to the decomposed state of the body, he had been unable to determine the blood group of the dead woman.

The last witness of the day was decorator and professional dancer Robin Robert Taylor, who claimed to have met Notyre in Sherry's Dancehall on 15 July. The two men had then moved on to an all-night restaurant where Notyre had, for reasons best known to himself, written on a card, 'The geezer talking to the plainclothes copper is a mouthpiece'.

Having got that off his chest, Notyre and Taylor had made their way to the flat in Kemp Street. Taylor, like others before him, had commented on the smell and was assured it was coming from upstairs. After Notyre had collected a suitcase and a black overcoat from the flat, the men had headed back to the all-night restaurant at around 4:30am. Notyre had then told Taylor he was anxious to catch the first train to London, adding, rather ominously, that there would soon be news about Kemp Street and his picture was likely to be appearing in the newspapers.

Taylor said he last saw Notyre boarding a London-bound train at Preston Street Station.

On that note, the trial adjourned for the day.

The trial resumed with the testimony of seventeen-year-old Doris Irene Saville, concentrating on her bizarre first encounter with Notyre in London and his attempt to draw her into his freshly concocted alibi. When asked by Cassels whether Notyre had told her why he wanted her to back up his story, Saville replied, 'He said he wanted someone to stand by him in court and that I could save him.'

Mr Birkett, clearly believing the girl to be an important witness, went on the attack. 'You are very different in appearance today from what you were on Sunday 15 July, are you not?'

'Yes,' Saville replied.

'Is it true that on that day you were dressed to appear like a woman much older than a girl of seventeen?'

'Yes'

'You were with a woman named Sally. How old would she be?'

'In her twenties.'

'Where is Sally now?'

'I do not know, I haven't seen her since,' the witness replied.

Birkett pushed on. 'Did anyone suggest you make yourself look older?'

'I did not intentionally make myself look older.'

'I put it to you that the prisoner said he was going for a bus ride, that you said, 'Wouldn't you like to take me?' and that he said you could go if you liked.'

'No, he asked me,' was the firm response.

'I suggest you did not go to Lee Green but to Lee, which is in the Bethnal Green district.'

'I thought it was Lee Green,' the girl meekly replied.

'I suppose you do not know where Lee Green is?'

'No.'

Warming to the task, Birkett pressed on. 'Your memory is not very clear about what happened that day is it?'

'Yes,' came back the faltering reply.

'Had you read in the papers about the trunk murders?'

'Not before I met Mancini.'

'Did you say to him, 'How could they get a woman's body into a trunk?' Now, think very carefully, may you have said that and forgotten it?'

'I don't think so,' Saville replied.

'Did he say, 'I don't know,' and did you then say, rather jokingly, 'You seem to know rather a lot about it, you are not the man, are you?' Is that not what you said?'

'No, sir.'

Birkett was not for letting go and tried again. 'Did you say, as I suggest, 'I really think you are the trunk man?'

'No,' the girl replied.

Birkett then read to the witness an extract from evidence she had provided to the Police Court. 'On the way back on the bus he talked about murder. He did not say what murder. He said a murder had been committed and he was innocent of it and I was supposed to have met him.'

'You did not tell us that today,' Birkett sneered, 'probably you have forgotten. Were you intending to convey, and do you intend to convey, he was saying 'There was a murder and I am innocent of it and I want you to help me.' Is that what happened.?'

'Yes.'

'It is perfectly plain, is it not, based on the facts, that he was quite clear that he was innocent of the murder? That is plain is it not?'

'Yes.'

In conclusion, Birkett asked, 'I do not suggest the smallest impropriety, but you have been kept by the police, have you not, since that time, in various homes?'

With another predictable response of, 'Yes,' the girl's ordeal finally ended.

Birkett objected to the admission of a statement Notyre was alleged to have made to Chief Inspector Donaldson during inquiries into another matter on 14 July. (The statement had been given during 'The Girl with Pretty Feet' investigation when Donaldson was chasing down a report of a missing woman, Violet Kaye). After considering the matter, the Judge ruled the statement was admissible.

Mr Cassels proceeded to read the statement, in which Notyre had said he had first met Violet Kaye in London in August 1933 and, at her suggestion, had accompanied her to Brighton. Notyre had told the woman he had no money and the couple had lived off Kaye's earnings, though Notyre had claimed to have no idea from where she got the money. This arrangement continued until he found a job. Notyre claimed he had arrived home one evening to discover a note that Violet had left for him. The note said she had gone to live with someone who could afford to keep her. Notyre had believed this to be a man named Moore. He then claimed to have purchased a trunk in which to store Violet's clothes. He had signed off the statement with his real name, Cecil Lois England.

Another statement was then introduced, one Notyre had made following his initial arrest. This statement told how Notyre had returned to the flat and, having received no reply at the door, climbed through a window. He was greeted by the sight of Violet Saunders lying on the bed with a handkerchief tied around her neck and blood everywhere.

The reading of the statement continued, revealing that Notyre had claimed to have become frightened, as he had been convinced the police would blame him and he had no alibi. The prisoner had admitted he did not have the courage to inform the police and had, instead, bought a trunk to conceal the body. The statement had concluded, 'She was a prostitute. There were always men coming to the house at all times of the night. I did not kill her, as God is my witness.'

In reply to a question from Birkett, Chief Inspector Donaldson revealed that Notyre had previous convictions for stealing silver, stealing clothing and loitering with intent to commit a felony, but had no history of violence. The Chief Inspector also said Violet Saunders had previously been convicted of offences relating to prostitution.

The next witness to be called was Sir Bernard Spilsbury.

Spilsbury held in his hand a piece of bone, which he declared to be the exact piece that formed the depressed fracture of the murdered woman's skull. He opined that the fracture had been produced by a violent blow from a blunt object whilst the victim was resting upon some hard surface. Either end of the hammerhead presented in Court as evidence could, Spilsbury offered, if used with great violence, have caused the wound, with death likely to have followed within a few minutes.

Cassels asked the witness if death could have been due to morphine poisoning, to which Spilsbury replied, 'No.'

Birkett, fully aware of Spilsbury's glowing reputation, attempted to undermine the testimony. 'How long have you been in possession of the small piece of bone which has been produced here for the first time, on the third day of the trial?'

'Since the first examination.'

'Did it not occur to you that the defence might have been informed that in your possession was that small piece of bone?' Birkett asked.

'I am afraid it did not occur to me. The bone was not ready to produce at the time I gave evidence at the Police Court,' Spilsbury replied.

Birkett, like a dog with a bone, would not let go. 'Let me get this perfectly plain, you appreciate that no doctor for the defence was at the post-mortem?'

'I did not think anyone was, in this case anyway.'

'For a piece of bone, which has been in existence all this time, to be produced on the third day of the trial does put the defence in some difficulty, does it not?' Birkett asked.

'I do not think it would take anyone long to examine it and come to a conclusion,' Spilsbury replied.

Moving on, Birkett asked, 'You will concede there are many other possible theories available to explain the death of this woman?'

'Yes.'

'Take morphine, for example. Dr Roche Lynch has said he could not be sure whether a fatal dose of morphine had been taken. Assuming it was a fatal dose, could that not account for death?'

'If nothing else were done, certainly,' Sir Bernard replied.

'Can a person can get severe injuries to the head, be unconscious and recover?'

'Yes.'

'Postulated, these injuries from which you say a person may recover, plus a dose of morphine which is described as a fatal dose, could death be due to morphine although the injuries to the head are apparent?'

'Yes.'

'Do you agree that it is beyond all science and skill to say, in this case, the extent of the dose of morphine taken?'

'Yes.'

'Would it be fair to say that all that is known with certainty is that it was more than a medicinal dose of morphine?'

'Yes.'

Having reduced Spilsbury's answers to monosyllables, Birkett next got him to agree that a person under the influence of drink or drugs might trip over a stone brace at the top of the steps leading to the Park Crescent basement, lose consciousness and then recover before death supervened.

In an attempt to claw back some ground, Spilsbury said he did not think a fall onto a flat surface would produce a depressed fracture.

Birkett was not for letting up and asked Spilsbury to replace the piece of bone removed from the murdered woman's skull. He then passed the re-assembled skull to the jury and suggested to Spilsbury that if someone fell from the top step of the flight and landed violently onto the iron rail, it could produce such a depressed fracture. Sir Bernard though this theory to be impossible. Birkett pressed the witness to accept that a depressed fracture could occur in such circumstances, but Spilsbury reiterated that it could not cause the fracture that had been found on the skull.

Cassels attempted to rescue the situation, asking Spilsbury if a fall such as had been suggested would be likely only to result in injuries to the head. Sir Bernard replied that in such circumstances, he would certainly have expected to have found bruising on other projecting parts.

The Judge, looking to clarify the position for the jury, asked Spilsbury, 'Is it, in your view, possible for this woman, having received the injury which you saw and having gone through a period of unconsciousness, to recover sufficiently to go to the bed or undress herself or do other things of this sort?'

Spilsbury replied, 'I have said it is possible for it to happen after a depressed fracture, but in this case, it is quite clear it had not happened. If she had survived for any extent of time she would not have died from shock, she would have died from haemorrhage of the brain.'

Birkett remarked dryly, 'This is the very first time this has been suggested in the whole history of the case.'

The case for the prosecution having concluded, the trial was adjourned for the day.

Birkett began the case for the defence by addressing the jury directly. He strongly protested about the way the case had been portrayed in the press, claiming 'wickedly false' stories had been published. 'It is not merely unjust and un-English, it is a crime akin to murder, that when a man is charged, indeed even before he is charged, statements of that kind should be made.

Making sure he emphasised his next point, Birkett told the jury, 'The one crucial, supreme, paramount thing in the case, is that the Crown must prove beyond all reasonable doubt that the prisoner is guilty of murder. The submission I make is that they have failed in that duty.'

Turning his attention to the evidence provided by Sir Bernard Spilsbury, evidence he had attacked strongly during cross-examination, Birkett said this had differed from the evidence Spilsbury had given at the Police Court. During that testimony, Spilsbury had stated, 'In my opinion, the cause of death was shock, due to a depressed fracture of the skull produced by a violent blow from some blunt object. I have examined the hammer-head. The larger end of it is just such an object which could have produced such a fracture. The general size of the fracture corresponds pretty well with the size of the larger end.'

The barrister then referred to the evidence the jury had heard from Spilsbury the previous day when he had stated the fracture could have been made by either end of the hammer-head, but most likely by the smaller end. 'What do you think of that?' he asked.

Declaring that he did not believe the jury required any explanation from Spilsbury, or any medical expert for that matter, regarding a hammer-head, Birkett said, 'All I want to emphasise, at this stage, is that this is the central point of the case for the Crown. If it leaves you, as I submit it ought to leave you, in so grave a matter with the gravest possible doubt, the burden which is upon the Crown most plainly and most manifestly has not been discharged. My Lord will tell you that if you have come to that conclusion your duty is clear, to return a 'Not Guilty' verdict.'

Pressing on, Birkett advised the jury to be on their guard against evidence that was filled with inconsistencies and contradictions and that flew in the face of every single point proved in the case. He advised, 'The prosecution had a witness claiming the prisoner had said, 'I gave her the biggest hiding she had ever had in her life. I bashed her about from pillar to post,' and yet Sir Bernard Spilsbury has said there was not a sign of bruising on the body.'

Birkett declared that one undisputed fact was the concealment of the body and the lies told to cover it. Before he'd had the chance to consult with a legal adviser, Notyre had freely admitted, 'I got frightened. I knew they would blame me and I could not prove I had not done it.'

The barrister then put to the jury that it was a mysterious fact in the case that the woman had taken more than a medicinal dose of morphine, indeed it might be considered to have been a lethal dose. Birkett commended to the consideration of the jury that given the possible effect of the drug, she could easily have fallen down the steps and met with a projecting stone or a window ledge.

The next theory Birkett set before the jury was that

someone else could have committed the murder. The victim was regularly visited by men and the Crown had done nothing to explain the evidence given by Kerslake. The barrister recapped for the jury the evidence Kerslake had provided, regarding seeing the woman on the afternoon of 10 May, the very day the prisoner has said he had discovered the body. Kerslake suspected Kaye had been drunk or drugged. She had been very frightened and was leaning against a wall for support and her hands and face were twitching. Down the steps to the basement, at that self-same moment, had gone another man.

Admitting it was beyond his power to prove the woman had died at the hands of another, Birkett submitted that it could not be discounted. If someone else had committed the murder, then every other aspect of the case fell into place. There had never been the slightest breath of motive and Mr Cassels had studiously avoided mentioning its presence or absence.

Before he called his client to testify, Birkett revealed that the prisoner's real name was Cecil Lois England. The man had spent two and a half years in the Royal Air Force and had later become a waiter in a Leicester Square restaurant, where he had first met Violet Saunders. He had subsequently been induced to accompany Saunders to Brighton, sometime around September 1933.

Notyre, who would fidget with a rosary throughout his time in the dock, much to the annoyance of the Judge, was then examined by Birkett. He stated that he had lived in London with Violet Saunders, whom he had known as Violet Kaye, for a period of about one week. The couple had then moved to Brighton, where they had lived at a number of different addresses. The longest time they had spent at any one address in Brighton had been about six weeks.

'She was a loose woman and I knew it,' Notyre declared. He went on to state that men had visited the woman at all the addresses they had lived in and there were four he could remember visiting the property at Park Crescent. The only two he could name were Charlie Moores and a man they called 'Hoppy', due to his being lame.

Birkett asked, 'So far as money is concerned, all the time you were in Brighton, from September 1933 until May 1934 when you obtained work at the Skylark Cafe, who provided all the money for food and pocket money?'

'She did,' Notyre replied.

'Did you earn anything at all?'

'No.'

Questioned further, Notyre claimed that the woman seemed to live in a state of constant fear. Some evenings she would come home and tell him to quickly pack up their belongings. They would move from place to place, never staying for long at any one address.

Birkett asked if Violet had ever taken drugs. Notyre replied that she would regularly drink to excess. He said Violet had kept a small bottle in a drawer in her room, but she did not know what it contained. Sometimes she would become depressed and she would say, 'It's alright, I know what I shall do.' She would then go into her room and fetch the bottle from the drawer. Notyre denied buying morphine for the woman or giving it to her at any time.

'During the whole time you lived with her as man and wife,' Birkett asked, 'how did you get on together?'

Notyre gulped and hesitated momentarily, before replying, 'Strange as it is, I used to love her. We were always on affectionate terms. There were no quarrels.'

'Did that cover the whole time?'

'Yes, every second she was alive,' Notyre replied, stepping up his performance with a stream of tears.

Notyre said he remembered Violet coming to the Skylark Cafe on 9 May. He had served her with food and they were perfectly happy and friendly. On 10 May, Violet had staggered into the cafe and had appeared to Notyre to be troubled by something. She'd left the cafe at around 3:30pm. Later that day, when he'd returned to the property in Park Crescent at about 7:30pm, Notyre said he'd had to climb through the first-floor window, as he had forgotten his key and had not received a reply when he had rung the front door bell.

Continuing his story, Notyre said that when he had finally got inside the flat, he had found Violet's coat lying on the floor of the bedroom. He'd then seen Violet lying on the bed, clutching the sheets with one hand. There was blood on the pillow and Notyre had checked the woman and found her heart had stopped beating. He had covered Violet's body with her coat and it was only then he'd seen a pool of blood between the door and the head of the bed.

Birkett asked the blindingly obvious question, 'Why did you not go to the police?'

'I am not going to make a long statement. I consider that a man who has been previously convicted never gets a fair and square deal from the police.'

'In what respect did you fear you would not get a square deal, was it because of your convictions?'

'Because I thought they would say, 'Very well, you must be the man, you have been living with her. You are a convicted man and you found her body."

Notyre said he had decided his only course of action had been to hide the body until he could, if possible, discover who had killed the woman. He had folded the bedclothes around Violet's body and had carried it to the front left-hand cupboard. After putting the body into the cupboard, he had knocked a long steel nail through the door with the heel of his shoe, fastening it shut. Notyre claimed never to have even seen the hammer produced in Court.

Notyre had then, he said, spent the night in an armchair. The following morning, he had found a letter in Violet's handbag which had indicated that her sister, Olive Watts, was due to visit. He had quickly arranged for a telegram to be sent that read, 'Going abroad. Good job. Sail Sunday. Will write – Vi.'

Stating that he had returned to work at the Skylark Cafe on 12 May, Notyre revealed he had taken Miss Attrill to Sherry's Dance Hall that evening. On the spur of the moment, he had offered Attrill some of Violet's clothes. The following night, he had taken Attrill to the Regent Dance Hall before taking her back to his flat. He'd explained the lack of bedclothes by saying he had given them away. He had then given Attrill a green costume, black coat, fawn hat and a pair of white gloves.

Birkett again asked the obvious question, 'Did you provide any explanation as to why the clothes were available?'

'She said it was very strange that Violet would have gone away without these clothes, which were almost new. I said she could not get them into her case. I had to say something.'

Notyre told the Court he had bought the trunk on the evening of Monday 14 May and had squeezed the body into it. He had then used some oil to cover the stains in the cupboard. On 15 May, he had hired a handcart and had moved the trunk to the property in Kemp Street.

In reply to another question from Birkett, Notyre claimed never to have said he'd had a 'dust up' or a 'tiff with the wife'. He did admit to having told several people his wife had gone to Paris but denied telling Joyce Golding that his wife had nagged him. He also denied saying, at Aladdin's Cave, that he had given his wife the biggest hiding she had ever had or that he had bashed her about from pillar to post.

Moving on to the statements he had given to the police in Brighton, Notyre said some of what he had said at the time had been untrue. He had given the statements because he was being pressed as to Violet's whereabouts and he had to make some excuse. He had been sure the police were watching and following him on the morning of 15 July. He had walked to Preston Park Station, to avoid going to the main station, to catch a train to London.

Birkett then asked Notyre about his meeting with Doris Saville upon his arrival in London. Notyre said he had not tried to make arrangements with the girl for her to come to his aid should he ever be charged.

The barrister then asked, 'Did you ever say anything to her about there having been a murder done and you were innocent of it?'

'No Sir,' Notyre replied.

'Or about you coming back and finding a woman dead and seeing three men, anything like that?'

'No Sir.'

'Or that you wanted somebody to stand by you in court if you were had up for murder? Is there any truth in that?'

'No.'

'Were you in any way responsible for the death of Violet Kaye?'

'I was not Sir.'

'Did you at any time use violence to Violet Kaye?'

'No Sir.'

'Did you ever use the hammer which is exhibit eleven in any way at all, let alone hit a woman with it?'

'I have never seen it.'

'Have you anything to do in any way whatever with the death of the woman you lived with?'

'No Sir.'

No doubt underwhelmed by the riveting answers Notyre had provided, Mr Cassels began his cross-examination.

Asked by the prosecutor why he had not called for assistance when he had found the woman dead on the bed, Notyre replied that he had been afraid.

'Afraid of what?' Cassels asked.

'Because I was afraid, as it is proved now Sir, I would be blamed for it.'

'And perhaps for good reason,' Cassels goaded.

'There was no reason.'

'Are you seriously asking the jury to believe you did not call the police because you consider that a man with convictions never gets a square deal?' the barrister asked in an incredulous tone.

'I am.'

'Have you ever been convicted of any crimes of violence?'

'That makes no difference.'

'Your suggestion is that the police would not have given you a square deal?' Cassels asked again, labouring the point somewhat.

'I am sure of it,' was the predictable response.

Finally moving on, Cassels asked Notyre if he had ever told Joyce Golding he had received a letter from Violet Saunders. Notyre denied having said this and was then asked if he could suggest any reason why the woman would have said he told her this. 'I have a good idea. Of course, I may be wrong, but I have a good idea,' Notyre teased. 'Miss Golding and Miss Gordon, being prostitutes living in Brighton, they, I say, have been asked to make damaging statements against me.'

Trying to steer Notyre away from his conspiracy theories, Cassels asked if he had told Miss Tinn that when he left Kemp Street it would become famous. 'Not in those words,' Notyre said. 'I told her I was going to London and she said she would not go if she were me. I said I must go back and if I did not, I would not be able to go anywhere at all. She said she did not understand and I said I could not explain. I then said to her that if I did explain, the whole of this place would be notorious.'

Cassels then asked Notyre about his claim Violet had appeared to be living in fear of something. Notyre replied that when they had first arrived in Brighton, two men had called on her. They'd subsequently moved to another address, but the men had called again at the new flat. About three weeks later, the couple had been walking along the seafront when a young man had come at them and had slashed Notyre's face with a razor. The man had then tried to slash Violet. Notyre claimed he'd knocked the man out. The man had then got up and run away.

The saga continued, with Notyre claiming to have gone to his good friends in the police force to tell them he was being blackmailed and required protection. The police told him that unless he could provide some proof he was being blackmailed they were unable to help, so he'd let the matter drop.

At that point, an end was called on the day's proceedings and the trial was adjourned.

The trial resumed with testimony being taken from two witnesses for the defence, Violet's former showbiz partner, Kay Fredericks, and Notyre's mother, Lydia England. Both claimed to have witnessed Violet, on occasion, appearing to be under the influence of drugs.

These were the last two witnesses to be called.

Birkett then began his final address on behalf of the defendant, pointing out to the jury that because he had called witnesses for the defence, he was compelled to speak first and would have no knowledge of what Mr Cassels was going to say in reply. He then imparted his heartfelt wish that sometime soon a reform would take place to allow the counsel for the defence to always speak last, so they may be in a position to reply to everything that was said.

Having removed this 'bee from his bonnet', Birkett said, 'I reaffirm, as the keynote of everything I desire to say, that the only question, in this case, is, has the Crown proved to your reasonable satisfaction that the prisoner at the bar killed Violet Kaye in that basement flat?'

The barrister then laid out his case before the jury. The prosecution's claim was that Notyre had taken a hammer and killed the woman, yet they had provided absolutely no explanation as to what his reason could have been for doing so. Birkett stated his belief that the prosecution's entire case had been basically destroyed by their failure to provide any motive for Notyre committing murder. It had been established that the couple had been on friendly and affectionate terms. It had only been after the event that Notyre had been alleged to have made statements that could be considered incriminating and the Crown had laid stress on these statements. Birkett asked the jury to bear in mind that what had been presented were allegations of what had been said by his client, not 'evidence of reality'.

Birkett claimed the case was riddled with doubt. He then declared his astonishment at the fact his client had not be asked a single question by the prosecution regarding the morphine found in the woman's body. This had been a greater than medicinal amount of morphine and may even have been a fatal dose. The barrister advised the jury that the two matters of motive and morphine should be enough to give them such misgivings as to make them say they had not been satisfied beyond all reasonable doubt.

Moving on, Birkett asked the jury to consider whether Notyre would have been likely to have held onto the hammer-head on which Sir Bernard Spilsbury had provided evidence. If he had used it to commit a horrible crime, would he not have been more likely to have got rid of the hammer-head, perhaps by throwing it into the sea.

The next seed of doubt Birkett tried to sow in the minds of the jury was whether someone else had committed the murder. That Violet had been a prostitute and that Notyre had lived off her earnings was not in doubt and Birkett conceded he had no words to say to the jury in extenuation or justification. What he did ask the jury to bear in mind, was that these circumstances had brought the couple into contact with a class of men and women belonging to an underworld that would make the minds of ordinary people reel.

The prisoner had already made it clear that the couple had

been required to move hurriedly from their home in fear. They had also been subjected to an attack from a razor-wielding thug. Birkett asked the jury if, in light of these events, it was too much of a leap for them to consider that a reasonable probability was that blackmail may have formed a considerable part of the dreadful and unspeakable life of the victim.

Somewhere out there were the people Kerslake had overheard speaking in the flat on 10 May. News of the murder had been shouted from the rooftops, Birkett said, so why has no one who was in the flat that day come forward. Did that not raise doubt in the minds of the jury?

In conclusion, Birkett said he believed he was entitled, by every principle of law known to the British system of jurisprudence and by every fact put before the jury, to do more than appeal for, but to demand a verdict of 'not guilty'.

Mr Cassels replied on behalf of the Crown, firstly pointing out that it was not necessary for the prosecution to prove motive. If the jury were satisfied Notyre had killed Violet Kaye it was not necessary for them to come to any decision as to what his motive may have been.

Turning to the hiding of the body, Cassels offered that such conduct was contrary to all human instinct and human nature, except in a case where the reason for the conduct was an overwhelming sense of guilt. Notyre's claim that he did not go to the police because he did not believe a man with a conviction could get a square deal from them held no water with the barrister. Was the jury really going to believe Notyre hid the body so he could solve the crime himself? He had called in no assistance, no doctor and had spent the night removing every trace of the crime before hiding the body in a cupboard.

The first thing Notyre had done the morning after the murder, was to take the precaution of stopping Violet's sister visiting the flat, as had been previously arranged. He had then purchased a trunk to hide, then move, the body and had then got rid of the woman's clothes.

If the jury were to give any credence to the story of the mysterious men that had visited the flat on the day of the murder, Cassels asked that they also consider what a wealth of information the prisoner could have provided if he had only called for assistance. Instead, he had gone down the route of destroying evidence and hiding the body.

Attacking the claim from the defence counsel that Violet could have died from morphine poisoning, Cassels pointed out that Sir Bernard Spilsbury had said this had definitely not been the cause of death.

Cassels finished his closing statement by saying that if all the evidence had led the jury to conclude the prosecution had proved their case then, painful though their duty may be, it was clear what it should be.

Mr Justice Branson began his summing-up by advising the jury of their need to disregard anything and everything they may have read in the newspapers or heard outside the Court and to base their decision solely upon the evidence that had been presented.

The Judge went through the background to the case once more for the jury, before addressing the question of motive. He impressed on the jury that it was no part of the law that the prosecution had to prove motive for a murder before a prisoner could be convicted. Before convicting, a jury only had to decide that the prisoner had committed the crime and the motive, as such, was quite irrelevant.

Sir Bernard Spilsbury had told the Court the cause of death had been a depressed fracture of the skull and the small dose of morphine found in the woman's body could not have caused death. The Judge told the jury that if they were not satisfied the woman died from the blow to her head, then he thought they should immediately acquit the prisoner because the Crown's case had been built around this premise.

Justice Branson then turned his attention to the suggestion some other person or persons unknown had gone to the basement, murdered the woman and left her body there. The jury had a duty to consider the suggestion and give it such weight as they thought right in conjunction with the rest of the evidence in the case, taking into consideration the actions of the prisoner in the matter.

According to Notyre, he had gone home and found the woman dead, put her body in a cupboard and nailed the door shut. 'What do you think of that as the actions of an innocent man?' the Judge asked. He then informed the jury to give all the weight they thought proper to Notyre's claim that having been previously convicted, though not of any violent offence, he could not rely on getting a fair deal from the police and had to, therefore, conceal the body. 'Can you imagine an innocent man dealing in this way with a woman he loved?' the Judge asked.

'Is it the action of an innocent man,' the Judge continued, 'who comes and sees a woman lying on the bed with a bump on her head, or do you think he would have summoned help and tried to get a doctor with the hope of being able to resuscitate her?' In coming to an opinion upon that question you will form your own estimate of the intelligence of this man.'

The Judge then asked that the jury, having seen the man in the witness-box and having heard the way in which he had dealt with the questions put to him, make up their own minds as to whether it was reasonable to credit Notyre with the folly of trying to hide the body, with all that entailed, unless he himself was the person who had killed the woman. Once he had chosen to hide the corpse, the Judge ventured, Notyre had no option but to lie to explain the woman's absence and this, in the Judge's view, meant the various stories he had told and the question of who was telling the truth in the evidence provided by Miss Saville was rendered moot.

Moving on to the statements Notyre had been alleged to have made in Aladdin's Cave, Justice Branson asked the jury to consider how likely it was that a murderer who had left the body of the victim and the murder weapon at the scene of the crime, would say to comparative strangers that he had 'sloshed her out with a hammer'. The Judge's view of that part of the case was that it favoured the accused.

Regarding physical evidence, the Judge pointed out there was no bloodstained clothing upon which the jury could rely on as having been worn by the prisoner on 10 May. They had no evidence as to what the prisoner had been wearing on that day except that which Notyre himself had provided. There was also no evidence except that provided by the prisoner as to the time of death. The Judge pointed out that nobody other than Notyre had seen Violet Kaye between 4pm on 10 May and the time when her body was found in the trunk in July.

Following the conclusion of the Judge's summing-up, the jury retired to consider their verdict at 1:50pm. Two hours and fifteen minutes later they returned from their deliberations.

When asked to deliver the verdict, the jury foreman rose and declared, 'Not Guilty.'

An eerie silence descended on the courtroom as people looked at each other in the hope of making sense of what had just happened. Notyre stood transfixed, his hands clamped around his head and his eyes betraying a state of incomprehension. It was left to Justice Branson to unfreeze time and announce to Notyre, 'You are discharged.' With a slight nod of his head, Notyre descended the steps leading from the dock a free man as the newspaper hacks rushed out to write their headlines.

On the back of 'The Girl with Pretty Feet' case, this was a disaster for the police and Chief Inspector Donaldson. The case had appeared to be a slam-dunk, the body had, after all, been found in the home of the accused. Statements made by the accused man himself, forensic evidence, witness statements and a confession to the concealment of the body had led the police to believe they had their man.

The main lesson to be learned was that under the British jury system, a top-quality defence counsel could, against the weight of the evidence presented, ensure there was no such thing as a guaranteed 'Guilty' verdict.

Notyre, maintaining his classy lifestyle, would go on to have a brief stint touring as 'Tony Mancini, The Infamous Brighton Murder Man', before eventually, and thankfully, disappearing from public view.

In 1976, Notyre finally confessed to the murder of Violet Saunders. In an attempt to squeeze money from his notoriety, he gave an exclusive interview to the News of the World under the headline, 'I've Got Away with Murder'. In this version, he claimed to have killed Violet after she had come at him with a hammer during a blazing row. He had, he revealed, taken the hammer from her then thrown it back at her, hitting her on the temple.

Of course, for Notyre telling the truth was an alien concept and a few year later he sold a different account of the murder to another newspaper. In this version, he claimed to have pushed Violet's head against the stove.

With no prospect of a retrial on the murder charge, on the grounds of double jeopardy, the Crown considered bringing perjury charges against Notyre. This proposal was eventually dropped due to a lack of corroboration because of the time that had passed. Many of those involved in the original case had since died and several case files had been destroyed.

Why anyone would still want to speak to the man is a mystery, but several years later, shortly before his death, he was back in the newspapers claiming he had been entirely innocent of the murder. Perhaps, as he approached death, Cecil Lois England, alias Jack Notyre, Tony Mancini, Tony English, Hyman Gold, Luigi Pirelli and Toni Luigi, was worried about having to face the judgement of a far higher authority. In any case, he would slither out of this world as an innocent man in the eyes of the law.

7 THE OLD CURIO SHOP

Even in the present day, Cecil Court, which links Charing Cross Road and St Martin's Lane, looks like a London street from a bygone era. Dating back to the seventeenth century, it is one of the oldest thoroughfares in Covent Garden. Due to its associations with the early days of the cinema industry, it had at one time been nicknamed 'Flicker Alley'. Since the nineteen-thirties, it has become known as Bookseller's Row.

In the year 1961, London was all set to 'swing', as was Edwin Albert Bush, the twenty-one-year-old offspring of a Pakistani father and English mother.

Number 23 Cecil Court was a quaint antique shop owned by Louis Meier, specialising in the sale of rare African and Egyptian antiquities and curios. In keeping with the others in Cecil Court, the little shop gave the impression of having stepped out of the pages of a Charles Dickens novel. The interior was dark and atmospheric and the walls were adorned with skulls, shrunken heads, voodoo dolls, ceremonial daggers and other such esoteric items.

Elsie May Batten was the wife of the world-famous sculptor Mark Wilfred Batten, who had been the President of the Royal Society of British Sculptors since 1956. The Batten family had their main place of residence in Castletown, West Kensington.

Mrs Batten helped fill her day by working part-time in her friend Louis Meier's shop. By 1961, the woman had been working in the shop for around two years and generally worked between 9am and noon, at which time Meier would take over.

On 3 March, as the rush hour raced by on the adjacent streets, Mrs Batten strolled down the City of London's own 'Sleepy Hollow' to open the curious little shop as normal. Unfortunately for her, the day was to prove to be anything but normal.

When Louis Meier arrived at his shop, at noon, to relieve Mrs Batten, he was surprised to find the paraphernalia normally on display outside the shop was not yet in place. Meier entered the shop but saw no sign of his friend Elsie. With a growing feeling of dread, he drew back the curtain leading to the back room and stood aghast as his eyes fell upon the prone body of Elsie Batten.

Meier quickly regained his composure and phoned the police.

Detective-Inspector Pollard was assigned to the investigation and was soon examining the crime scene. A ceremonial dagger protruded from the woman's chest and another was firmly embedded between her neck and shoulder. Yet another dagger could be seen underneath the body and a heavy stone jar lay nearby. It was clear to the policeman that as well as her other injuries, Mrs Batten had sustained a severe blow to her head.

Mrs Batten's handbag was lying close to her body but there was nothing to indicate the bag had been ransacked. The impression of a heel print could be seen on a piece of board beneath the body.

The visibly shaken shop-owner was asked if he was aware of any items that may be missing from the shop. Meier looked around then told the policeman he was only aware of one, a ceremonial sword.

Scotland Yard issued an appeal, saying they were anxious to speak to anyone that had passed through Cecil Court between 9:15am and 11am on 3 March or had visited the area on the previous day. The little self-contained street was ideal for the police to carry out door to door inquiries and they had soon spoken to every shop-keeper in the vicinity.

Following the initial local enquiries, the investigation spread. Over the course of the next few days, the police visited all other antique dealers around London.

On 6 March, Scotland Yard announced they were looking to trace a young Indian male who had been known to have visited several antique shops around the West End and had been enquiring about a specific type of Indian dagger. The man had been seen in the company of a young girl, who was described as 'blonde with a ruddy complexion and thought to be aged around seventeen years old'.

Detective-Sergeant Raymond Dagg, who in a happy coincidence had just recently completed a course on the subject of Identikit, put together a drawing of the lead suspect. The Identikit drawing Dagg produced was based on descriptions provided to him by two separate witnesses. Dagg ventured back and forth between the two, giving them access to the widest range of features available in the Identikit before contenting himself that he had produced the best possible likeness of the suspect. The drawing was then released to the press.

The Identikit was a device developed by legendary lawman Hugh McDonald, a Los Angeles detective, in 1959. The kit was made up of drawings of distinctive head shapes, noses, chins, eyes, lips, hairlines, eyebrows, beards, moustaches, spectacles, wrinkles and headwear. Based on descriptions provided to the user of the kit by witnesses, the various features were pieced together to form an accurate reconstruction of the face of a suspect.

Identikit would subsequently be replaced by Photo-FIT and E-FIT, though the general principle would remain pretty much the same throughout.

Armed with his copy of the Identikit drawing of the chief suspect in the Elsie Batten murder case, Police-Constable Cole was out pounding the beat in Old Compton Street when he spotted a man who bore a close resemblance to the one in the drawing. The fact the man was in the company of a young blonde-haired girl was the clincher for the constable. After conducting a brief interview with the couple, Cole detained the man for questioning.

On 9 March, Edwin Albert Arthur Bush, aged twenty-one, a labourer from Ewart Road, Forest Hill, was charged at Bow Street police station with the murder of Mrs Elsie Batten. Bush was remanded in custody until 17 March and granted legal aid due to his lack of funds.

Evidence was taken on 5 April, at Marlborough Street Magistrates Court.

The first witness to be called was twenty-one-year-old Janet Edna Wheeler of Floyd Road, Charlton.

Wheeler explained that she and her boyfriend, Edwin Bush, had gone to London's West End to purchase an engagement ring. While the happy couple had been lost in a conversation concerning the planning arrangements for their forthcoming engagement party, they had been interrupted by a policeman. Following a brief interview, the policeman had taken Bush into custody.

Wheeler continued, stating that she and Bush had only shortly earlier been discussing the recent murder in Cecil

Court. Having read a newspaper report on the two people the police were seeking in connection with the murder, they had laughed heartily about the resemblance they bore to the descriptions in the article.

Mr Peter Palmes, who was leading the prosecution, then rose and went over the events that had occurred on the morning of the murder.

Palmes said he believed that Mrs Batten had opened the shop sometime between 9am and 9:15am. During that morning, fifteen-year-old Peter King had called into the shop and had seen what he thought was a dummy lying on the floor behind the curtains at the rear of the shop. When he noticed the fingernails of the 'dummy' were painted with red nail varnish he then thought a woman may have fainted. Rather than investigate further, the confused boy had left the shop.

When Louis Meier had arrived, between noon and 1pm, he'd spotted that pictures and prints that should have been on display outside the shop had not been put out. On entering the shop, he had found the body of Mrs Batten.

Palmes continued, stating that on the day prior to the murder, Mr Meier had been alone in his shop when an Indian man, accompanied by a girl, had come to inspect an antique sword. Later that same day, a nearby gunsmith, Mr Roberts, had been visited by an Indian man who had asked him if he would be interested in purchasing an ornamental sword.

The following day, the Indian man had returned to the gunsmith's shop and had offered to sell a sword. The sword had been wrapped in brown paper. Mr Robert's son had been serving behind the counter at the time and he'd asked the man to return later to discuss the potential transaction directly with his father. The man had left the sword in the shop but had subsequently failed to reappear.

Based on the descriptions provided by Meier and Roberts, it had been clear they had dealt with the same man.

An Identikit drawing had been put together by Detective-Sergeant Dagg. The drawing had then been widely circulated, together with a statement saying the man may have been seen in the company of a young blonde girl.

Police-Constable Cole, while on patrol in Old Compton Street, had spotted a young couple fitting the description and had asked them to accompany him to Bow Street Police Station. During his discussions with Cole, Bush himself had commented on the resemblance he bore to the face in the Identikit drawing.

Bush and Wheeler had informed the constable they were out looking to buy an engagement ring, valued at sixteen pounds. Given that Bush had no money or employment at the time, Palmes ventured that it was not clear from where he had intended to obtain the money for the purchase.

Palmes went on, stating that an impression taken from the heel of Bush's left shoe was a perfect fit for the print left on the board found next to the body of Mrs Batten.

It was then revealed that, in a statement he had provided to the Police, Bush had admitted visiting the curio shop and asking Mrs Batten to wrap up a sword he had looked at earlier in the day. Bush had told the woman he would return to the shop later to collect the item and pay for it.

Bush had indeed returned to the shop and, after inspecting various daggers that were on display, had picked up a nearby ornament and struck Mrs Batten on the head with it, knocking her to the ground. As she had attempted to get back onto her feet, Bush had hit the woman in the stomach, stabbed her in the neck with a dagger and then plunged another dagger into her heart. He had then run from the shop.

Bush had concluded his statement by saying, 'I am sorry I did it. I don't know what came over me. Personally, I think the world is better without me. I am very sorry about the whole thing.'

Later, Bush claimed he had only provided the statement because the police said they had something on his girlfriend and suggested his statement would make things easier on her. This takes a bit of believing, given the graphic nature of the statement and the likely consequences of his confession.

Bush's sister, Iris, was then called on to offer her testimony. Iris told the Magistrate she had met with her brother on 2 March and had accompanied him to the shop in Cecil Court. Bush had intimated to Iris that he would like to buy a sword that had taken his fancy, though Iris said the sword in question was not the gilt-handled ceremonial sword shown to her in Court.

After leaving the shop, Iris had said to Bush, 'You know you haven't got the money to buy a sword. How do you think you are going to get it?' Bush had replied, 'I'll get it somehow.' Iris had ended the conversation by advising her brother not to do anything stupid.

The following morning, Bush had informed his dumbstruck sister that he had just hit an old lady in the shop up the road and, although he had not meant to do it, he thought she'd 'had it'.

Louis Meier was next up. Meier said that on the eve of the murder, Bush had come into the Cecil Court shop and told him he wanted to buy a present for his girl. Meier had leapt to the assumption Bush was referring to the girl who was accompanying him at the time, but that had, in fact, been his sister Iris. Bush had asked Meier the price of a dress sword hanging on display, but had baulked at the asking price of fifteen pounds and had instead turned his attention towards a Saxon sword costing six pounds. Meier said Bush had then looked through a pile of daggers and had moved three of these to the top of the pile before leaving the shop.

Fifteen-year-old Peter King then took the stand to explain that he had gone into the shop to purchase a billiard cue.

King said, 'I walked halfway down the shop when I saw legs and a hand on what appeared to be a dummy. The leg had a bruise on it and there were red fingernails on the hand. I just waited for a few seconds and then came out again. I could not make my mind up about it later.'

Detective Inspector Harry Howlett stepped forward next and informed the Magistrate that Bush had told him he had never been in an antique shop in the area. Bush had also claimed to have a fear of handling knives, a phobia of which, he stated, his girlfriend was acutely aware.

Howlett then revealed that after being picked out in an identification parade made up of ten men, including several Indians, Bush had changed his story and had declared, 'The girl has nothing to do with it. I did it alone. I only took a sword. I took it to the shop opposite.' Bush had then signed a statement to that effect.

The Magistrate decided there was sufficient evidence to enable the case to be referred to the Central Criminal Court and Bush was formally charged with capital murder 'in the course or furtherance of theft'.

The murder trial, before Mr Justice Stevenson, opened on 10 May 1961.

Mr Griffith-Jones led the prosecution and opened by going over all the evidence put forward at the Magistrate's Court hearing.

Bush was finally allowed his say from the witness box on 11 May. He claimed he was not guilty of 'murder in the course or furtherance of theft' and had, in fact, lost his temper with Mrs Batten after she had directed an offensive racist remark towards him.

Telling the Court he had never regarded himself as being coloured, Bush said he tended to lose his temper when he heard anyone pass any abusive remarks with regards to the colour of people's skin. He went on to say he could remember striking the victim with a stone jar in reaction to the alleged remark but claimed to have no recollection of having stabbed her with the daggers, though he supposed he must have done so.

Continuing, Bush said he had become unemployed following an accident. As a result, he did not have sufficient funds to purchase the engagement ring he wished to give to his girlfriend, Janet Wheeler.

In reply to his lawyer, the wonderfully named Mr Christmas Humphreys, Bush said he had intended to raise the money for the ring by stealing the sword from the antique shop and selling it elsewhere.

Having first noticed the sword on 2 March, Bush had returned the following morning with the intention of stealing it. He was, he claimed, planning to distract the woman who was working behind the counter, then he intended to run off with the sword as soon as her back was turned. While he was haggling with the woman over the price of the sword, Bush claimed Mrs Batten had become angry and had exclaimed, 'You niggers are all the same. You come in and never buy anything!'

On being pressed by Humphreys, Bush said he had lost his head and hit Mrs Batten with his fist and then in a state of blind panic, he had struck her with the stone jar.

Mr Griffith-Jones asked Bush if he disputed stealing the sword, to which Bush replied, 'No.' The prosecutor then asked whether, between the time he had gone into the shop to steal the sword and the time he had come out, Bush had killed the victim with three daggers and the stone jar. Bush replied in the affirmative.

The trial was adjourned until the following day.

The next day, Judge Stevenson directed the jury to consider whether Bush had murdered Mrs Batten in furtherance of the theft of the sword. If they believed that was the case, it would be their duty to convict him of capital murder, which carried a death sentence. If the prosecution had failed to make the case for capital murder, but the Jury still believed Bush had killed Mrs Batten, their duty would be to convict him of murder.

After deliberating for over two hours, the Jury returned to reveal their verdict. Bush was found 'Guilty of the capital murder of Mrs Elsie May Batten.' The Judge declared that it was his view the Jury had reached the only possible verdict in the case and he proceeded to formally sentence Bush to death.

Police-Constable Cole was commended by the Judge, who said to him, 'You deserve the congratulations and the gratitude of the community for the great efficiency you displayed in recognising this man in the way you did. You were the direct instrument of his being brought to justice and your vigilance deserves the highest praise. I hope it will be clearly recognised by those in authority.'

A notice of appeal against the capital conviction was lodged in the Court of Appeal on 17 May and a hearing was held on 13 June, before the Lord Chief Justice, Mr Justice Ashworth and Mr Justice Salmon.

Mr Christmas Humphreys and Mr Richard Body appeared for the appellant and Mr Alistair Morton for the Crown.

The appeal had been brought on the grounds that the appellant had been wrongly advised by his counsel to plead guilty to murder. The appellant claimed to have killed Mrs Batten in an uncontrollable fit of temper as a result of being called a 'nigger'.

After hearing the legal arguments, the Court took the view the jury at the trial could not have shut their eyes to the fact that immediately after killing Mrs Batten, Bush had stolen a sword and gone to a gunsmith, where he had hoped to sell it. Whatever its significance, on an earlier visit to the curio shop he had laid aside three sharp daggers from a pile of knives. It appeared to the Court Bush had been obsessed with the idea of obtaining the sword and had gone to the extreme length of killing to get it.

The Court considered the trial Judge's summing up to have been fair and believed there had been ample evidence to support a verdict of 'murder in the furtherance of theft'. The appeal was, therefore, dismissed.

The Home Secretary felt he was unable to recommend a reprieve and on 6 July 1961, Edwin Albert Arthur Bush, aged twenty-one, had the unenviable distinction of becoming the last man to be hanged at Pentonville Prison.

From Scotland Yard's perspective, the case had been dealt with remarkably quickly.

The first use of the Identikit in Britain had been a major success and it must be said that the picture created by Detective-Sergeant Dagg was a pretty impressive likeness, although the unique look of the perpetrator must have helped.

The use of systems based on the principals of Identikit would soon become commonplace. Identikit would be followed by Photo-FIT and then various computer-based systems, including E-FIT. A modern-day replacement would come in the form of the circulation of images sourced directly from CCTV, though computer-generated portraits remain in use.

A relaxing of immigration laws, allowing unhindered rights to enter the country to people from within the Empire and Commonwealth who held British passports, resulted in mass immigration to Britain in the nineteen-fifties. The racial tension that accompanied the mass immigration was still firmly in place at the beginning of the sixties and many of those immigrants drawn by the offer of work in the 'Motherland' would encounter prejudice.

Racial prejudice was clearly not a mitigating factor in this case, though the constant descriptions of Bush as being an Indian, when he was actually the son of a Pakistani father and English mother, tends to show that the people of 1961 had not yet fully embraced the idea of London as the all-embracing multicultural and multi-racial city it strives to be today.

OTHER BOOKS BY THE AUTHOR

True Crimes: Ladykillers
The Curious Case of Charlie Peace
True Crimes in Victorian Times: Murder in Pocock's Fields
Edinburgh: A Capital City

Printed in Poland
by Amazon Fulfillment
Poland Sp. z o.o., Wrocław